I0813793

CAZA

CAZA

2011-16

CONTENTS

100 WALLS

IWAN BAAN

NEVER
GIVE
UP

Baptistry

RUDY
TIBASA

Chapel of San Pedro

SLIP LEFT THEN PUNCH RIGHT: ANTICIPATING VOLATILITY

CARLOS ARNAIZ

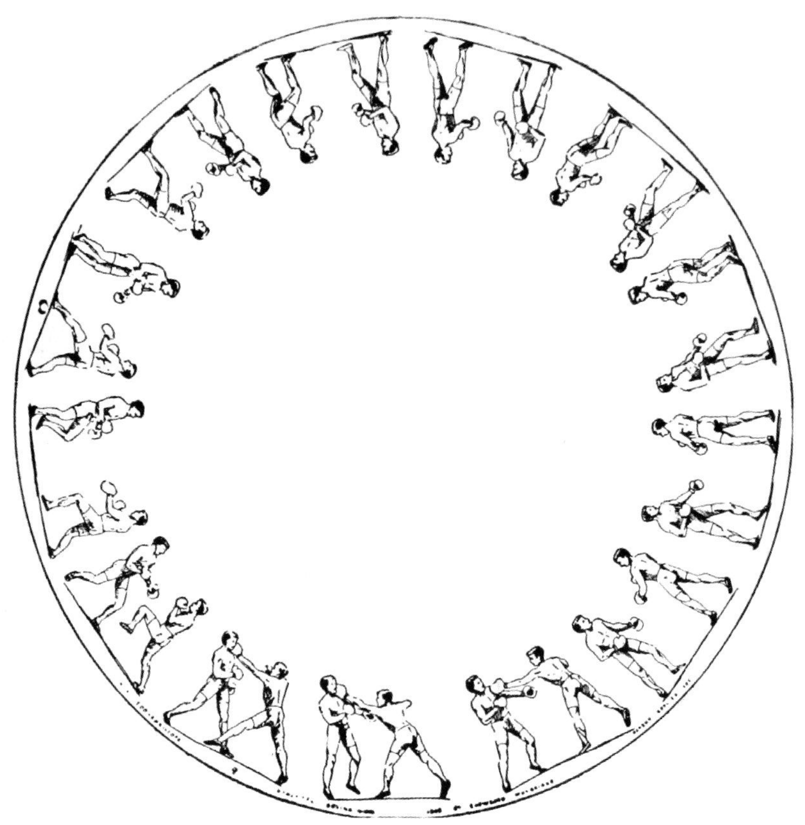

Athletes Boxing, Eadweard Muybridge, from *Zoopraxiscopy*, 1887

To gaze in on another may be an inadequate path to understanding, but in the case of boxing, it might be the only one.
—Christopher Bedford

Boxing is probably our earliest form of civilized combat. Considered to be one of humanity's oldest experiments in relationary dynamics, it pits two fighters in a ring bound by a set of rules. The Greeks held matches to commemorate the fallen after a war. The Romans popularized athletes as the most prized entertainers in the empire. The sport's drama is a function of a tightly controlled volatility: two bodies are throwing punches at each other with the intensity of serious conflict while the precipitating chaos is subject to strict spatiotemporal regulation.

A boxer-in-training, however, is confronted by none of these exigencies. Boxers train in an almost melancholic solitude, repeating a combination of moves devoid of the presence of the other boxer. They punch, slip, and block alone. They drill outside of the ring and typically box in front of a mirror. They gaze at themselves, attempting to imagine the missing boxer while confronting an optical inversion of their surroundings. A boxer's practice is a kind of perverse functional diagram by which a subject projects the possibility of a specific kind of relationship with another subject through their absence.

The ancient Hellenic sculpture *The Boxer of Quirinal* is a breathtaking homage to this process of partial and unfinished subjectivity. The Boxer rests. He is neither in training nor in a fighting stance. His genitals are scarred, his skin is cut, his hands are gently wrapped, and his slanted head bespeaks a history of vicious combat. We don't know if he is triumphant or in agony. His repose is not free of the ghost of the other boxer.

The Boxer's solitude suggests the presence of another body. We consummate the implied absence of his attacker by building an imaginary bridge between his body and the act of fighting. His scars, his straps, his exhausted muscles, all refer to something outside of the space of the sculpture. We envision the ring, his opponent, and the unpredictable frenzy of two bodies at war. The Boxer's solitude is a proxy for the tacit knowledge construed out of an incomplete picture of reality.

Critics liken boxers to dancers. The metaphor works because both dancing and boxing are radical forms of alternative communication. Professional dancers and prize boxers are obsessive readers. Their strength comes from their ability to be in extreme physical discomfort while remaining open to the shifting subjectivities of another body. Boxing technique is based on the need to interpret and anticipate volatility.

A boxer's form is rhizomatic. They slip left then punch right, flowing through a cycle of unbroken vectors that map out a system of tangent relations. They must imagine the body of their attacker while staring at themselves in a mirror. Boxers can only learn to cognitively flip their body for that of their attacker through relentless practice.

Boxing gyms are temples of repetition. The sights and sounds of these gyms are familiar to all boxers: a hypnotic rhythm of rings—three minutes on, 30 seconds off, three minutes on—with bodies moving through their combinations and punching objects that endlessly return. Repetition cultivates nerve sensitivities necessary for the dual processes of reading and reacting to volatility.

Boxers are in constant search of a partner to analyze and in turn self-evaluate. They must defend and attack simultaneously. Their posture and their split-second movements address the other boxer. Every punch must be connected to another move. Boxing is an example of technique over ideology in a situation of hyperconnectivity. Boxers learn how to act in a tense environment populated by another body whose unpredictable movements define their survival.

Architecture is similarly beset with issues of connectivity and social cohesion while being confronted with piecemeal conceptions of our universe. As architects, our practice is based on the critique of forms before they are fully crystallized. We are tasked to design for life that has yet to emerge. Our profession profits from the creation of spaces in the absence of people who will inhabit them. We perform interviews, conduct surveys, and host countless user group meetings in the hope that we can address this gap. Like the boxer, we must build future ecologies of chance while working with incomplete fragments of ourselves in the present.

Boxing as a model for design privileges the need to deal with change. Boxers must be watchful of what is not yet there. As architects, our work consists of a limited repertoire of operations meant to produce explosive outbursts of creativity. Our moves are simple and our technologies archaic. Like the combinations a boxer is taught, our tools consist of the rudimentary projection of matter into space. Boxing and architecture are practices that prosper by viewing the world wrong side up. The power of design rests in its capacity to transform the commonplace through a different appraisal of reality. Program, building materials, and site are subject to a permanent intervention of action. We are obsessed with techniques that produce an upturned diagram of the social futures we must anticipate. Our tools of projection present nature as both changeable and eternally in flux.

The boxer's effortlessness in the ring is our inspiration. We strive for a practice that never overcommits to a particular ideology. Extreme conditioning in architecture demands a loose scanning of our surroundings in the hope of finding alternative patterns of inhabitation.

The ideological battles of the last few decades can be summarized in terms of their neglect of technique. We must design navigable environments for the shifting sensibilities of users we don't know or who don't exist. Architectural form-making should never be absolute. We are, after all, practicing an applied sociology in the future.

Approaching architecture as spatial technique first before ideology enables us to reassign the making of form as the means by which we acknowledge our precarious state as beings continually threatened by near ruin. Our design techniques, like those of the boxer, are based on an admission of incomplete knowledge through active engagement. We must make do with the imperfect reality of our profession by focusing on how we make things in this world for users we can never fully know.

The body of the missing boxer is the strategic regulating factor in this relationship. The boxer construes the other body in the ring through a specific series of operations in space and time. His attack is conceived as a series of forms that adapts as it occupies time. The presence of other moving bodies in space triggers a pattern of proportions, distances, and volumetric overlaps. Geometry is hereby activated by use and charged with the ability to produce effects.

"If they give you lines offer them circles," a boxing coach tells his young pupil. Understanding thrust as a function of shapes moving through space is a boxer's technique for both defense and attack. Geometries calculated in relation to their potential for influence turns architecture into a method to both think and act. We can see our world, assess our failures, and devise delightful ways to make it work differently.

Architecture at a time of massive information overload demands a bias toward action. Why would one select a straight line versus a curve? The answer depends on our understanding of how forces affect a territory. Architectural technique requires us to be connected to our surrounding systems in a specific formal way. Our practice necessitates a continual evaluation of the shape and organization of these connections. Our work entails the construction of fractionally new worlds out of old recyclable forms.

Global production cycles force us to commit to the impossible. We are expected to innovate. Our industry values disruption. Novelty is our means of reacting to an environment that is defined by its ability to never stop. The current mediated design marketplace has brought about a situation of watered-down populist sleekness.

As architects trying to be in the vanguard, we don't truly know what we are doing—keeping this in mind is our strength and advantage. Geometry offers us a method to deal productively with our madcap desires. Major details remain in flux while we run toward tighter implementation deadlines. We are asked for magic so we must keep the illusion up. Like the boxer, we are compelled to diagram the unpredictable, to listen for the future movements of other bodies in this world and imagine new architectural configurations that bring about spaces between relaxation and efficiency.

Architecture is a spatial practice obsessed with relationships that might fail. Failure in the system is the reason we admire the boxer's effortlessness in the ring. Looseness with agility or strength with flexibility ensures that energy can be dispersed across multiple figures in a field of activity so as to enable the machine to reboot itself after a partial collapse. The correlation of points in the space, not the abstract volume of the space itself, is how failure is averted. It is a form of working that is as interested with what is physically present as with that which passes through a space. The boxer trains relentlessly to be able to see the transient eruptions of force in the ring. All that work helps him understand volatility and react accordingly.

Boxing and architecture offer a technique for intervening in the world by always watching for the logic of action outside ourselves. Our environment, our cities, and our communities are at stake anytime we choose between specific geometric patterns of action. Our capacity as designers rests in being able to gather entropic forces and create meaningful connections without cancelling out the reality of our precarious present. Design as an anticipatory relationship with others, albeit a kind of action-based ethics, offers up the possibility of civility as a physical and emotional aftershock to late capitalism.

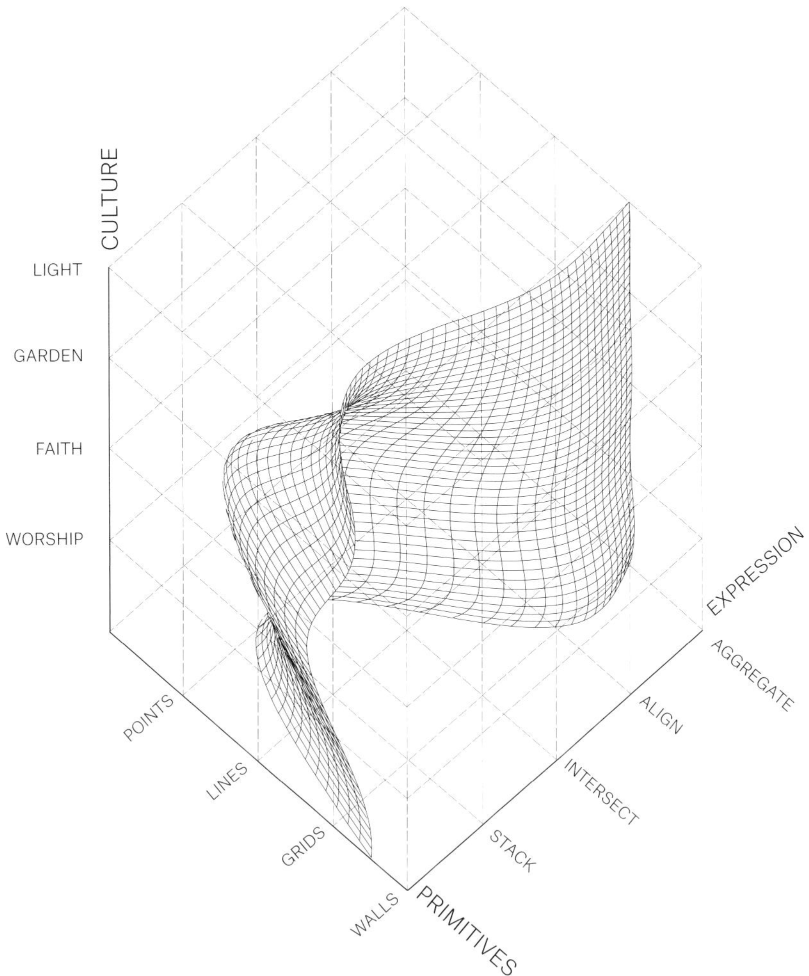

Plotting the 100 Walls Church along the axes of cultural utility, primitive geometries, and formal expressions

Wall inventory studying the effects of plan and elevation difference in the Church

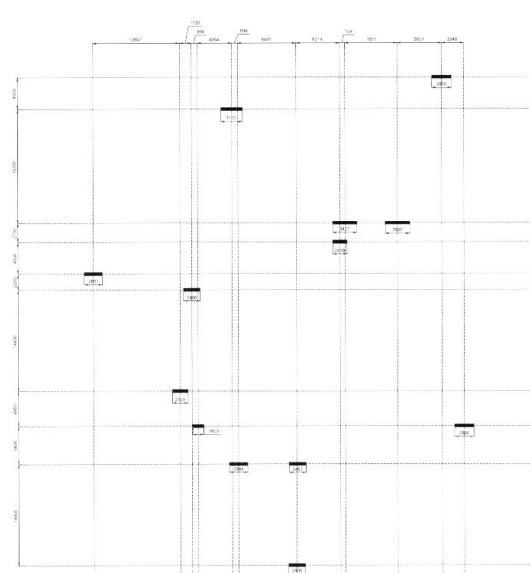

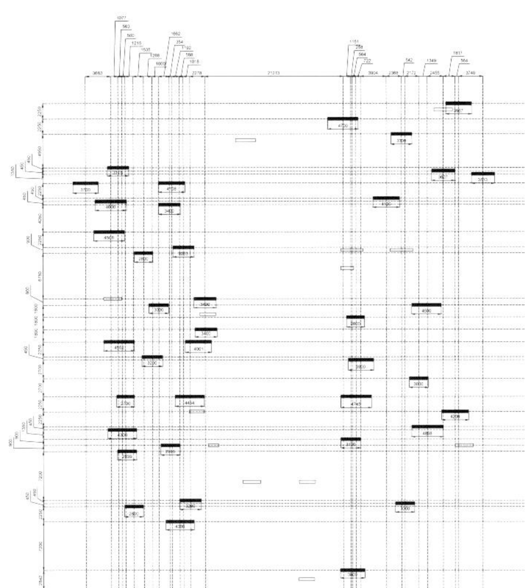

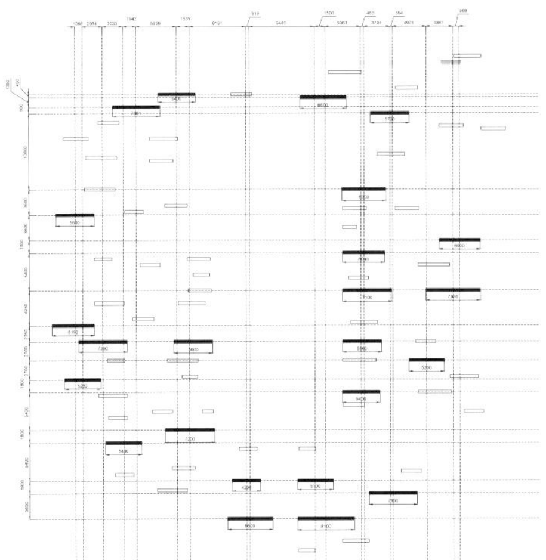

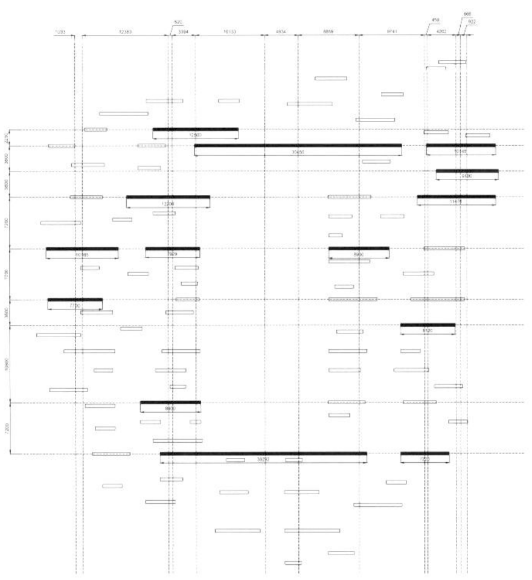

Vector diagrams linking the walls with the alignment of interior spaces

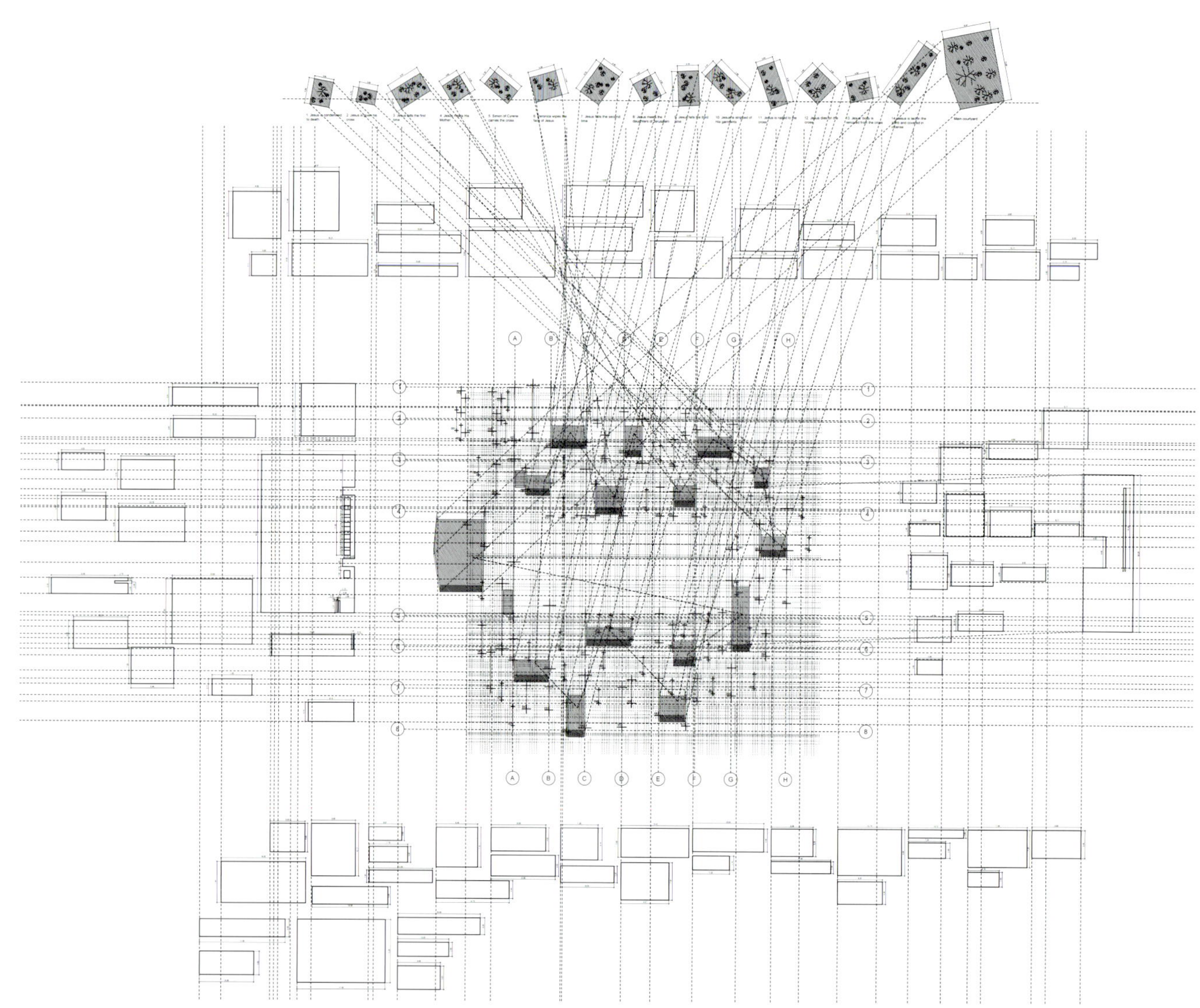

Narrating a spiritual experience through the Church with the use of 14 perimeter gardens

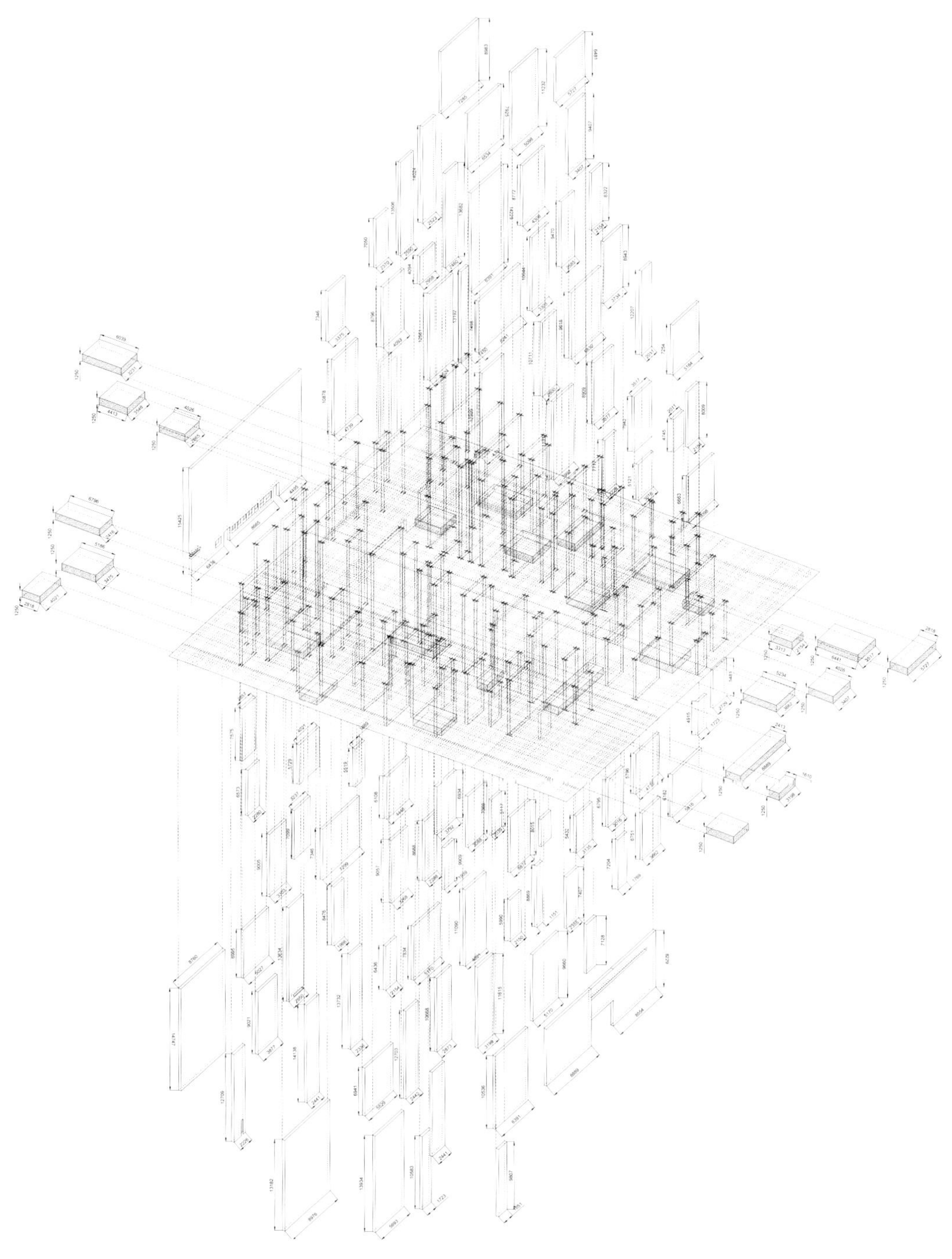

Exploded axonometric relating each wall to the ambulatory space and the congregational hall of the 100 Walls Church

COSTA RICA CONGRESS HALL

SAN JOSÉ, COSTA RICA

THE COSTA RICA CONGRESS HALL IS ORGANIZED AROUND A SERIES OF STRUCTURALLY DEPENDENT AND INTERCONNECTED CONCRETE-CAST HYPERCUBES CLAD IN STEEL LOUVERS. THE HYPERCUBES GAIN THEIR STRENGTH THROUGH PHYSICAL CONNECTIVITY. THIS FORMAL DUALITY DEMONSTRATES THE PRECARIOUS ROLE OF PUBLIC BUILDINGS IN TODAY'S WIDE-ANGLED DEMOCRATIC ENVIRONMENT. THE COUNTRY'S MYRIAD POLITICAL PERSPECTIVES ARE THE INSPIRATION FOR THE VERDANT HANGING LANDSCAPE OF SKY TERRACES COVERED IN LOCALLY SOURCED TREES AND PLANTS THAT ADORN THE EXTERIOR OF THE STRUCTURE. THE PROJECT'S COMBINATION OF GEOMETRY AND NATURE REVISITS THE LEGACY OF TROPICAL MODERNISM IN SOUTH AMERICA, INVITING THE CITIZENS OF COSTA RICA TO IMAGINE THAT ARCHITECTURE CAN BE A HOST FOR THE MEETING OF SOCIAL STRUGGLE AND ECOLOGICAL FANTASY.

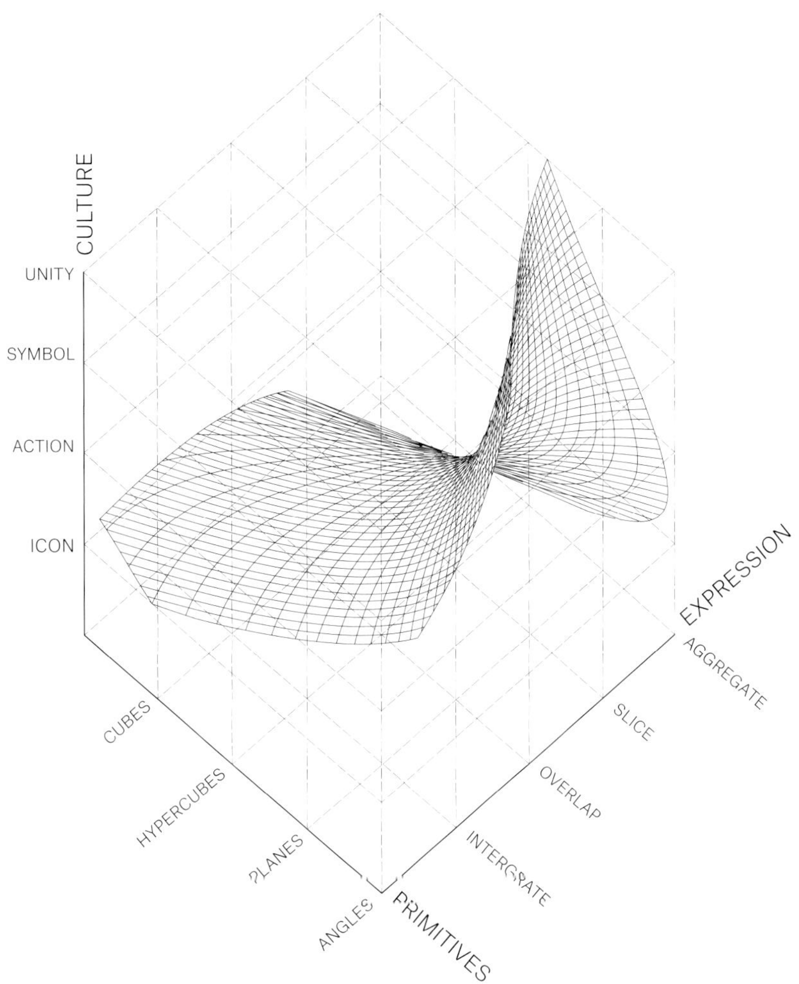

Plotting the Costa Rica Congress Hall along the axes of cultural utility, primitive geometries, and formal expressions

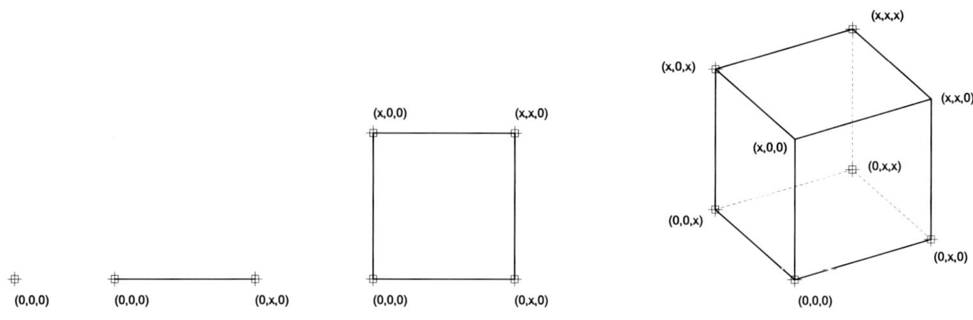

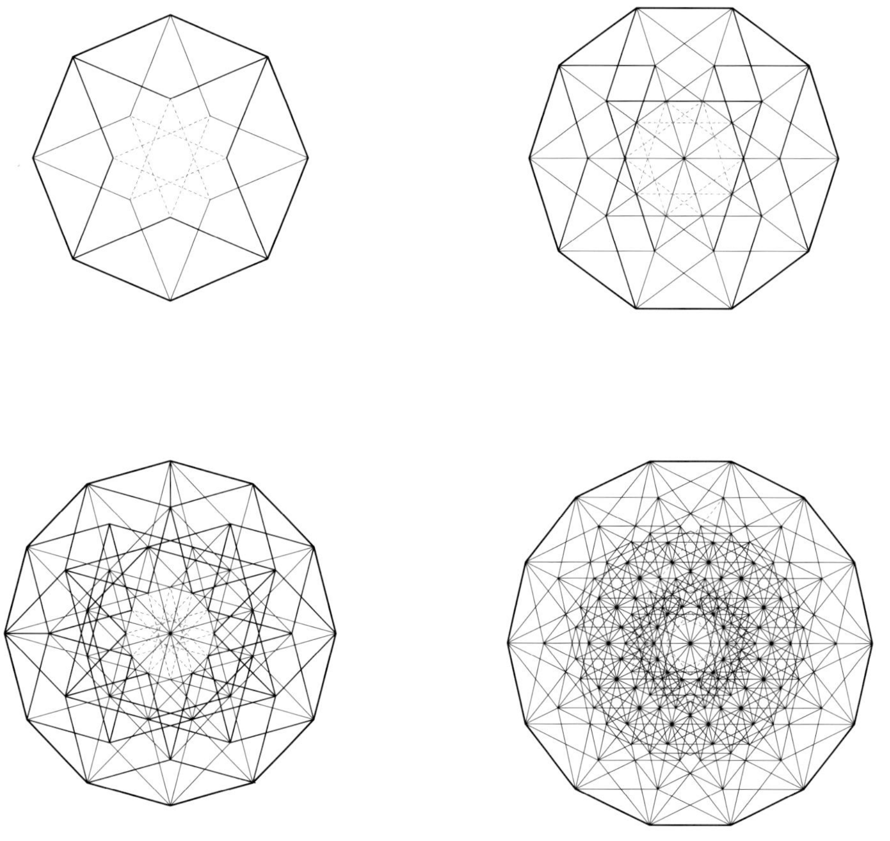

Studies into the compressive strength of compound polygons
spiraling out from a center

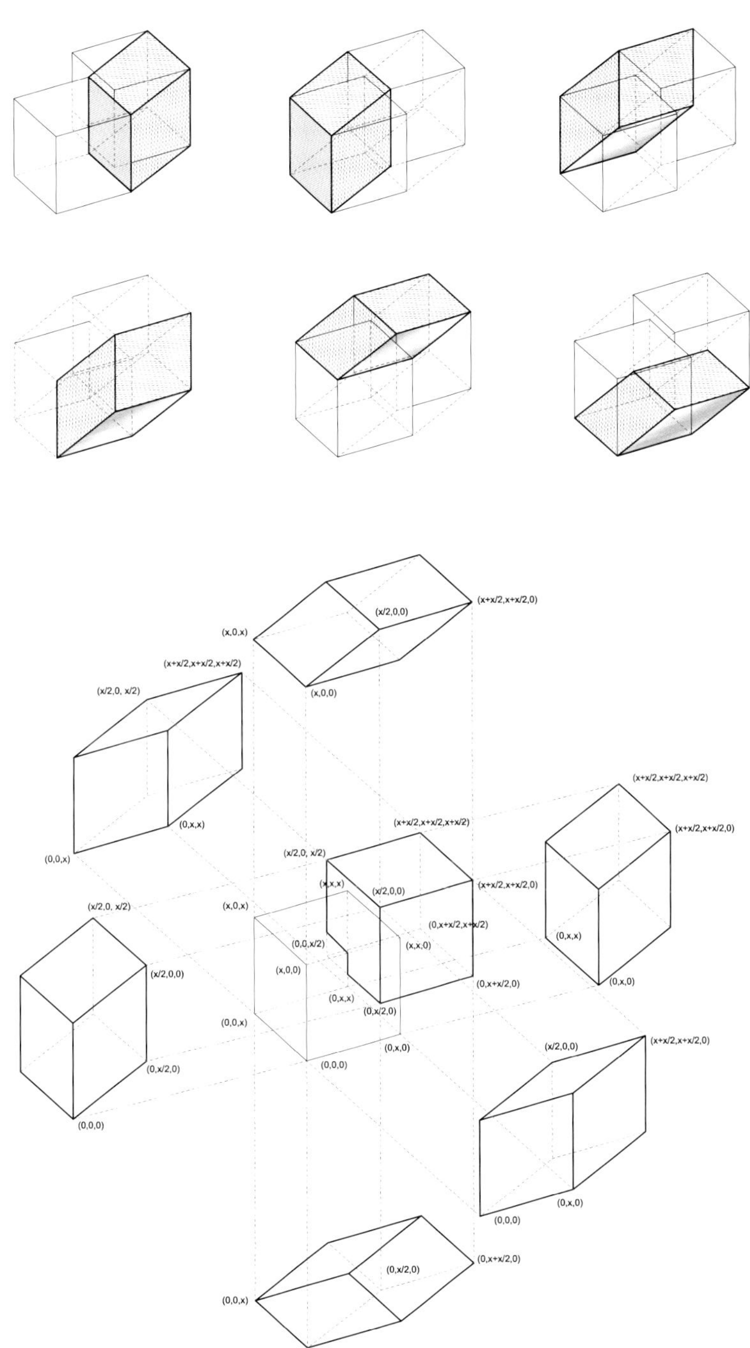

Diagrams showing how the conjoining of hypercubes produces interlocking spaces for the Congress Hall

Creating usable floor spaces from the intersection of multiple hypercube combinations

Exploded axonometric illustrating the relationship between the offices, the public terraces, and the circulation zones of the Costa Rica Congress Hall

CEBU TRANSIT

CEBU CITY, PHILIPPINES

AS A PART OF THE PHILIPPINES' FIRST BUS RAPID TRANSIT SYSTEM, CEBU NEEDED A SYSTEM OF MODULAR STATIONS THAT RESPONDED TO THE LOCAL CONTEXT WHILE PROJECTING THE FUTURE OF NEW CEBU. WE DESIGNED A ROOF AND CANOPY STRUCTURE BORNE OUT OF ONE FOLDING OPERATION WHEREBY THE HORIZONTAL AND VERTICAL SURFACES ARE GEOMETRICALLY MATCHED TO CREATE BUS STATIONS, WITH AN ALTERNATING SPATIAL BIAS FOR LOADING PASSENGERS AND DRAINING RAINWATER TOWARD RETENTION TANKS THAT KEEP THE ROADS DRY DURING THE WET SEASON.

THE DESIGN PRODUCES MAXIMUM OPPORTUNITY THROUGH A LIMITED SET OF ARCHITECTURAL MOVES, PAYING SPECIAL ATTENTION TO HOW THE STRICT PRAGMATICS OF INFRASTRUCTURE RESPOND TO THE CULTURE OF PLACE THROUGH AN EVOCATIVE SCREEN OF LOUVERS THAT ECHO CEBU'S LONG LEGACY OF TEXTILE PRODUCTION.

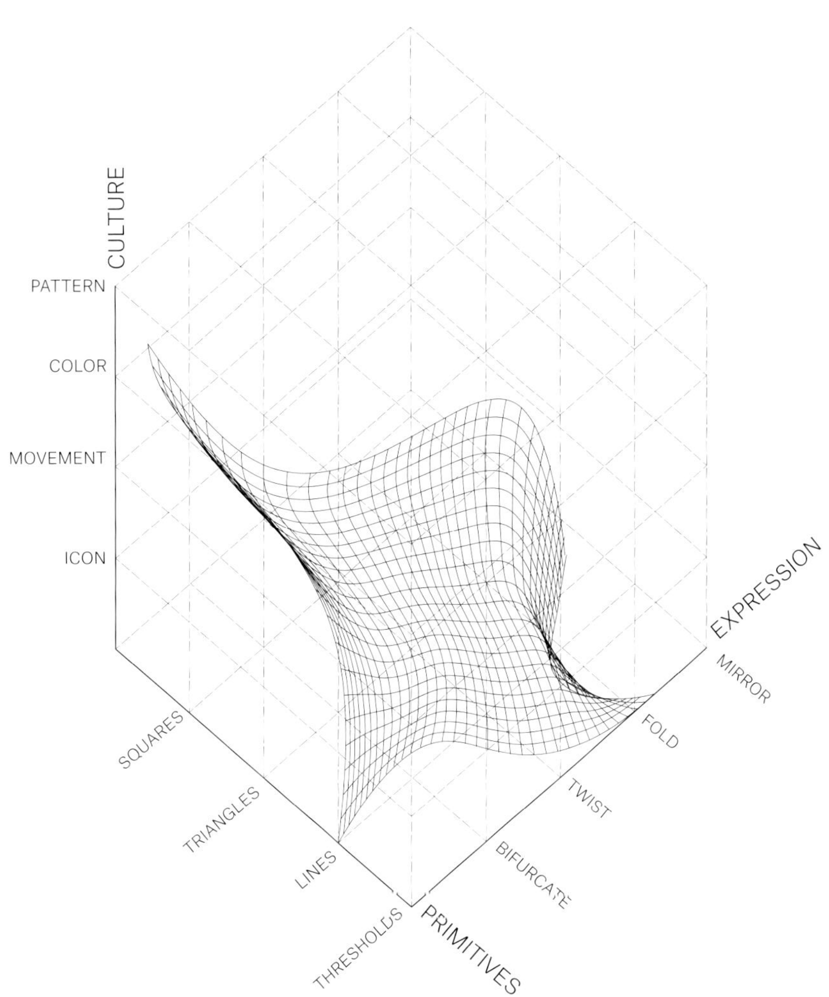

Plotting Cebu Transit along the axes of cultural utility, primitive geometries, and formal expressions

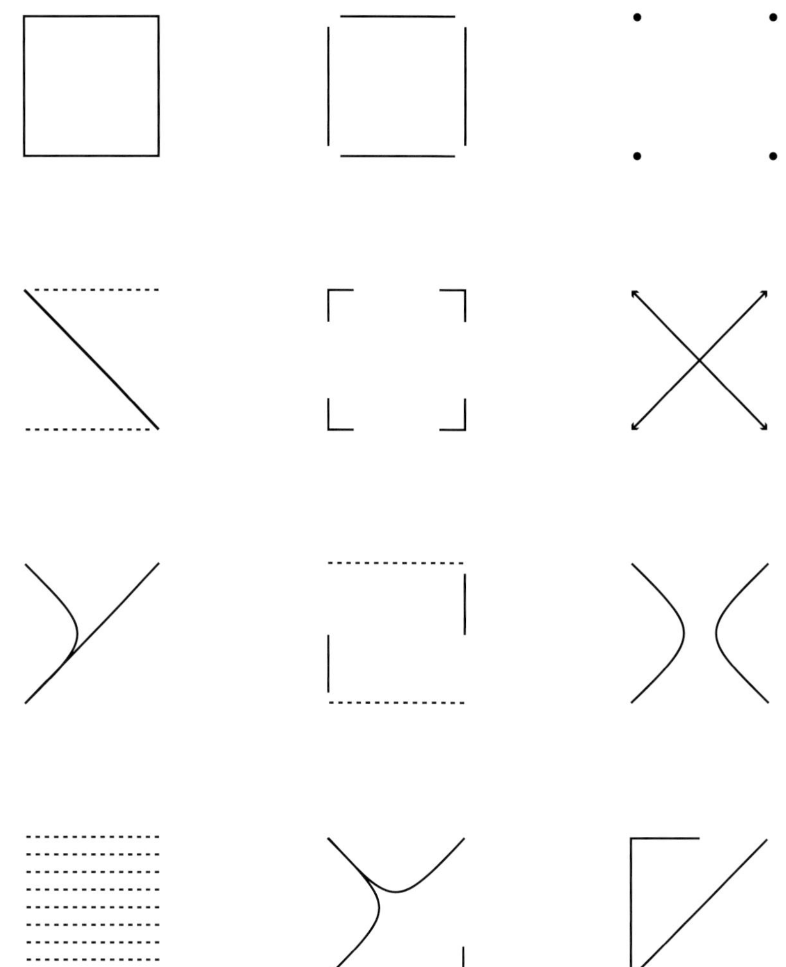

Studies for the development of the basic station module as a tool
to board buses and move out of the city

Diagrams looking at the extension of the modular into a linear series that responds to different environments in the city

Creating a folding template that makes roof and structure with one architectural move

Exploded axonometric showing the structure, skin, and ventilation louvers in a typical Cebu Transit station

HOUSE OF MANY MOONS

SANTA ROSA, PHILIPPINES

A SECLUDED RETREAT HOME OUTSIDE OF METRO MANILA, THE HOUSE IS A MEDITATION ON TWO MODES OF SEEING: TELESCOPIC, UP TO THE HEAVENS, AND TERRASCOPIC, OUT TO THE EARTH. VISITORS ARE PRESENTED WITH TWO TALL AND HEAVY STRUCTURES, CLAD IN NATURAL STONE, REGISTERING AN IMAGE OF A NEW TECHNO-TRIBALISM.

THE SOCIAL SPACES ARE ORGANIZED AROUND A LOW-SLUNG PENTAGON WITH A COURTYARD IN THE MIDDLE. THE BEDROOMS PIVOT AROUND A DRUM-SHAPED FAMILY ROOM, LOCATED BENEATH THE COURTYARD, THAT SERVES AS A COOLING CHAMBER. EACH BEDROOM HAS ENCLOSED PATIOS WITH MOON-SHAPED OCULI, WHICH OFFER A DISTINCT VIEW TO THE SKY, WHILE ALSO SERVING AS VENTING CHIMNEYS.

THE HOUSE SETS UP A COUNTERPOINT TO ITS SURROUNDING LUSH, TROPICAL LANDSCAPE THROUGH A CONSTELLATION OF CAREFULLY MANICURED GARDENS. THIS JUXTAPOSITION ENCAPSULATES THE DUALITIES INHERENT IN THE HOME: TO BE BOTH PRESENT AND DETACHED FROM THE SHIFTING GEOGRAPHIES OF OUR PLANET.

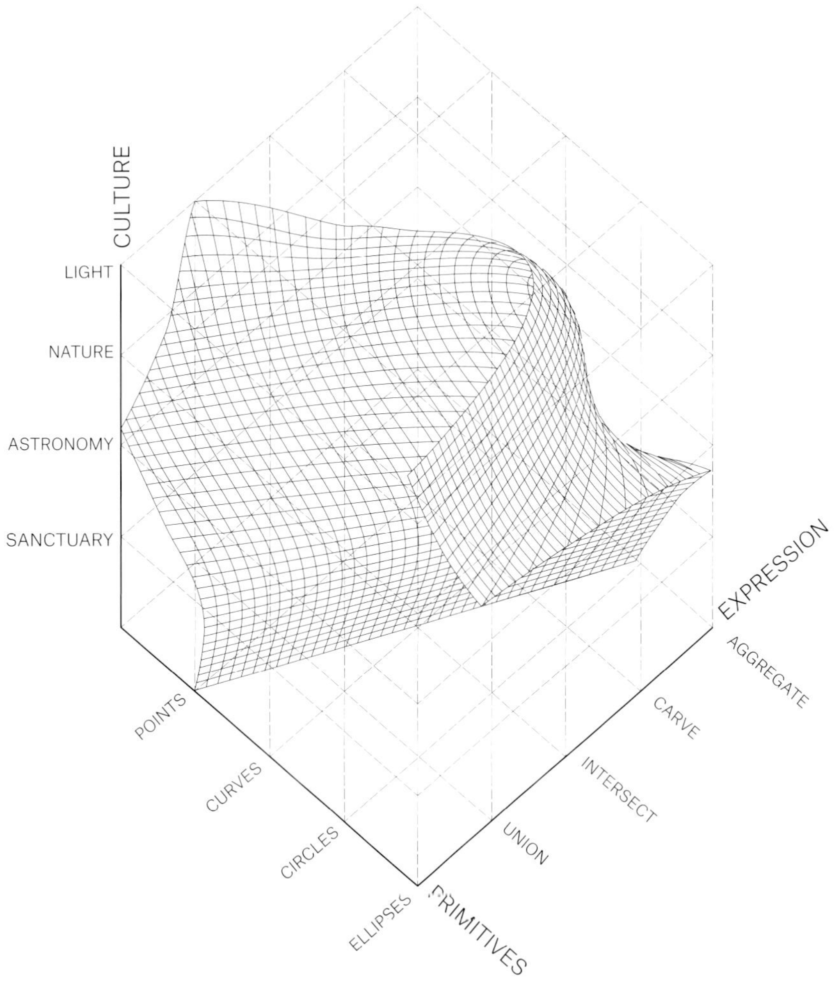

Plotting the House of Many Moons along the axes of cultural utility, primitive geometries, and formal expressions

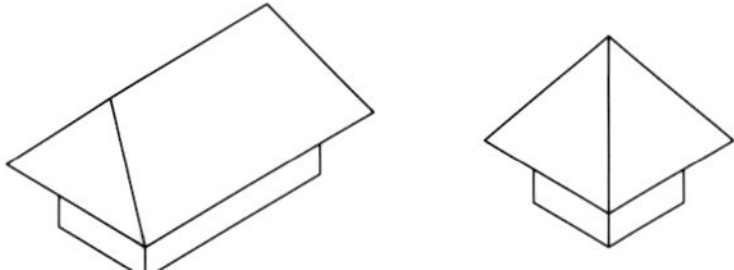

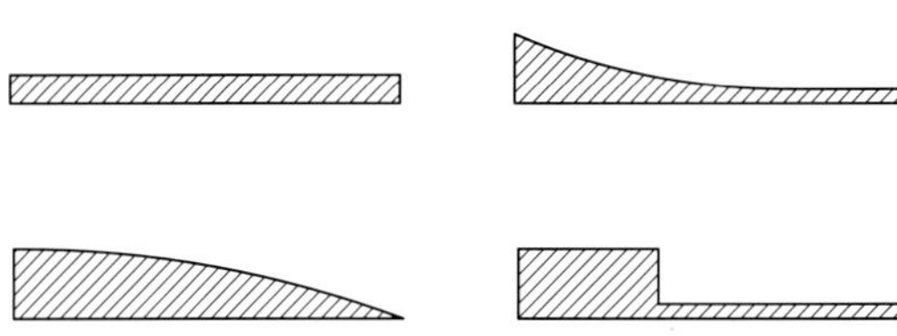

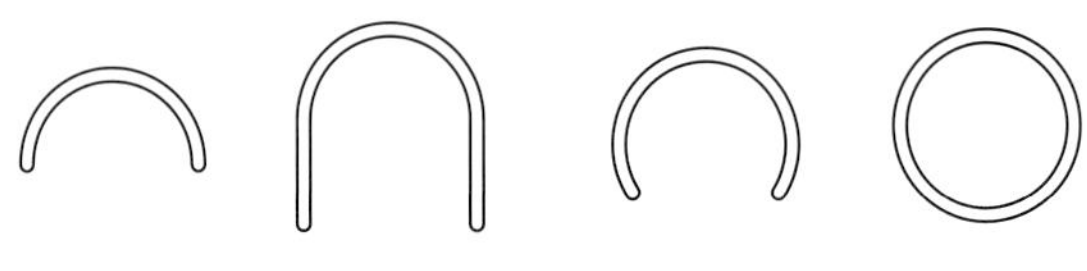

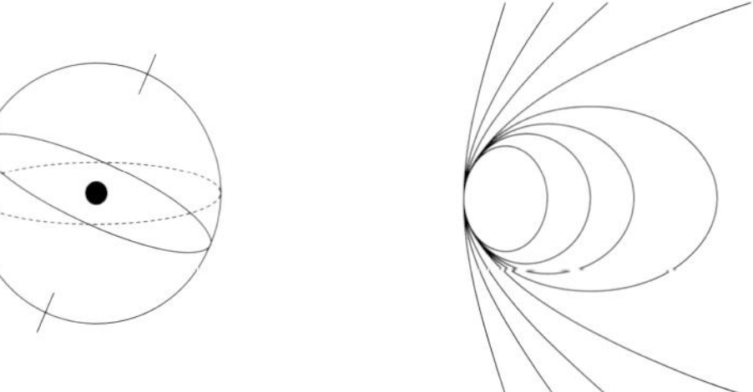

Studies exploring the telescopic and terrascopic apertures of the House

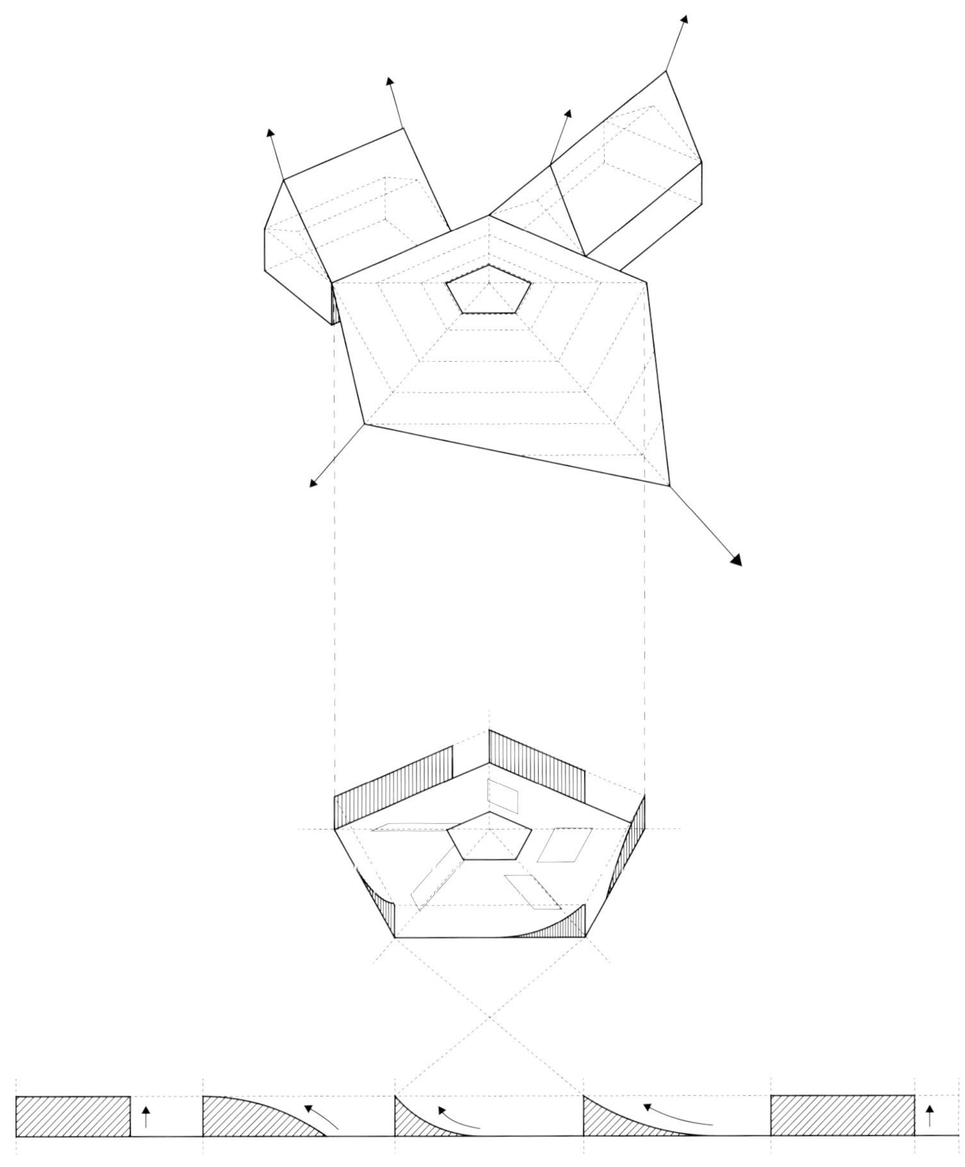

Diagrams illustrating how the terrascopic views inform the circulation through social spaces in the House

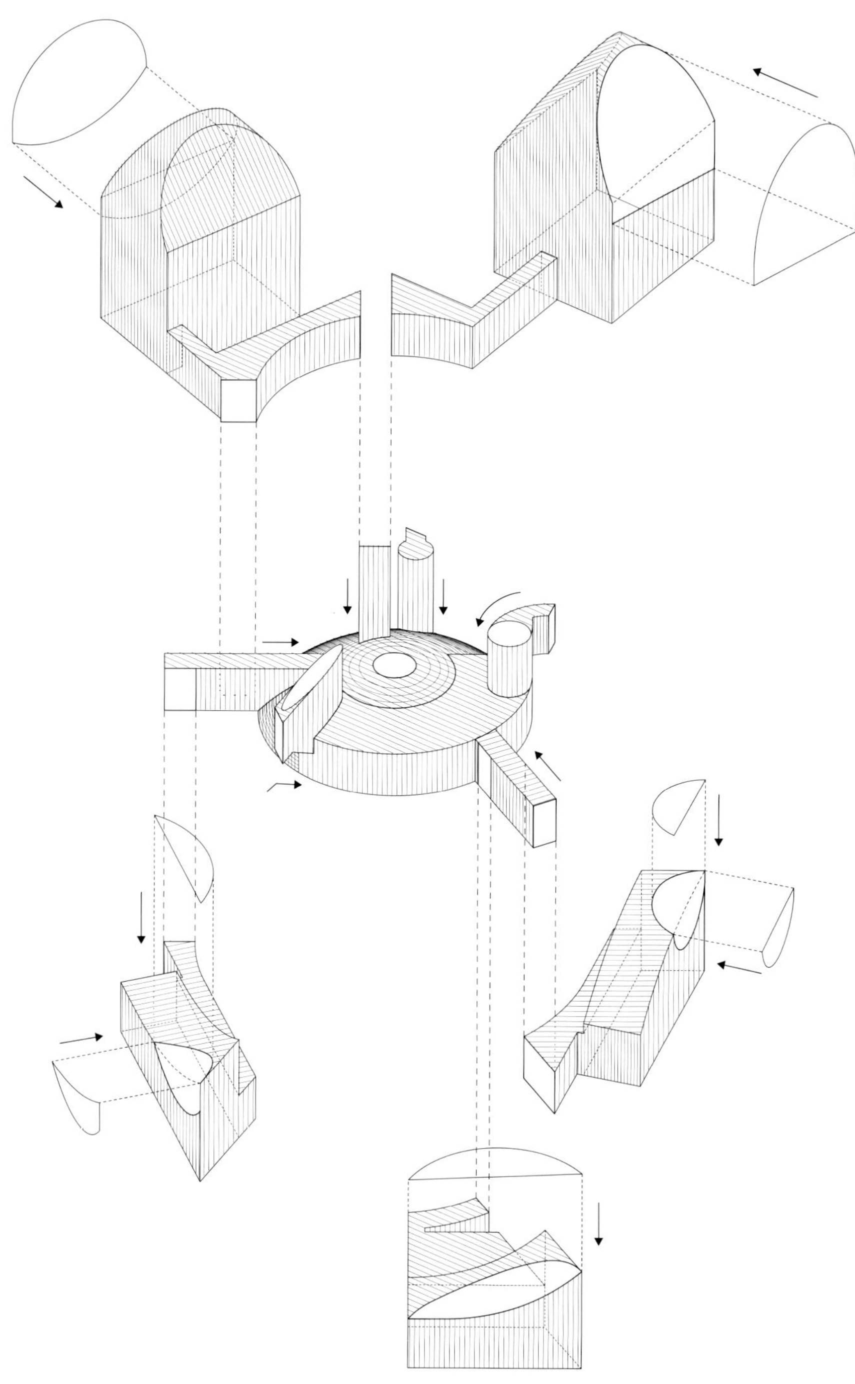

Connecting the central sanctuary and personal spaces of the House
with the moon-shaped oculi

Exploded axonometric illustrating how the patios of each bedroom look up to the sky through different telescopic shapes in the House of Many Moons

HAISHU WATERFRONT

NINGBO, CHINA

THE NINGBO HAISHU WATERFRONT DISTRICT IS AN ISLAND, SURROUNDED BY WATER ON ALL FOUR SIDES, OFFERING A UNIQUE TOPOGRAPHICAL SETTING IN WHICH TO REIMAGINE URBAN LIFE IN 21ST-CENTURY CHINA. CONTEMPORARY CHINESE CITIES HAVE ENTERED A NEW ERA OF 21ST-CENTURY URBANISM. OLD STRATEGIES FOR DEVELOPING NEW DISTRICTS NO LONGER WORK: CITIES CANNOT RELY ON INSTANT BUILDINGS, AND ICONIC PROJECTS NO LONGER BEGET THEIR OWN ECONOMIES. THE DESIGN OF THE WATERFRONT IS INFORMED BY DILIGENT ANALYSIS AND DRIVEN BY A THOUGHTFUL APPROACH TO MIXED-USE DISTRICTS, WHICH HAVE A RANGE OF SCALES DEPENDING ON THE INTENSITY OF THEIR SURROUNDING URBAN CONTEXT. DESIGNED ALONGSIDE A CAREFULLY CONSIDERED MODULAR GRID, THE MASTER PLAN TAKES INTO ACCOUNT THE SPECIFIC REALITIES OF THE TECH-DRIVEN ECONOMY: ITS MARKET TRENDS, PRICING PATTERNS, DEMOGRAPHIC SHIFTS, AND ECOLOGICAL IDIOSYNCRASIES. WITHIN THIS METROPOLITAN ISLAND, WE HAVE CREATED A VAST NUMBER OF POSSIBILITIES FOR HOW LIFE CAN UNFOLD IN THE CONTEMPORARY CHINESE CITY.

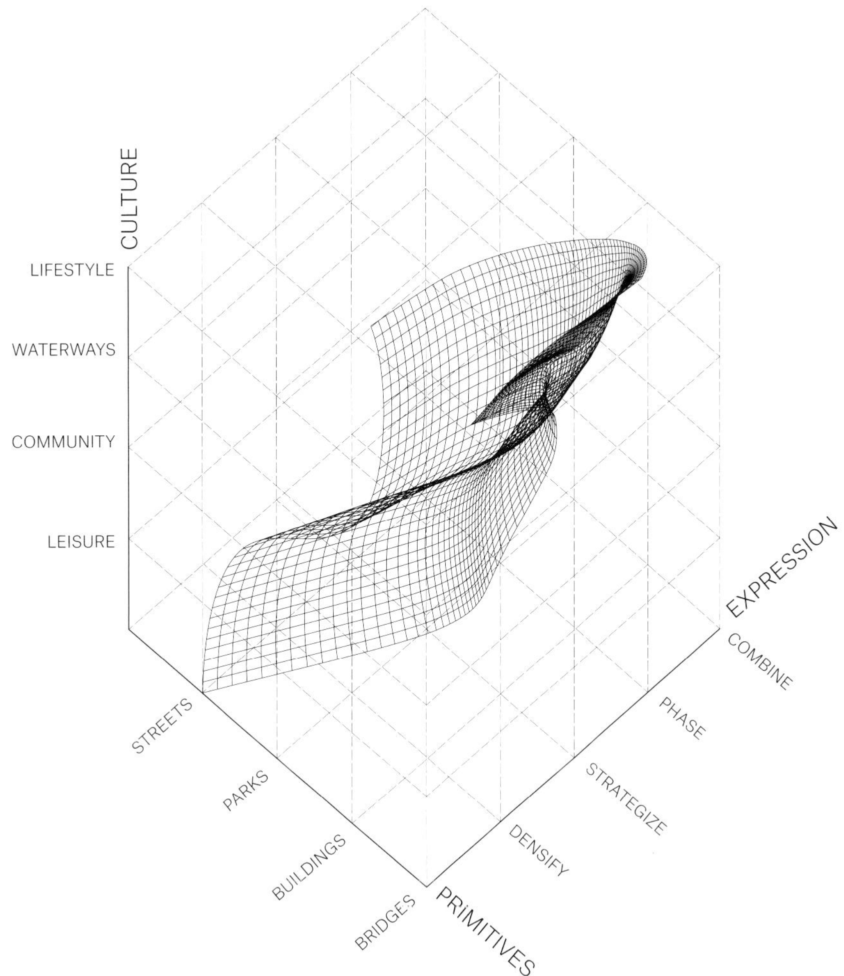

Plotting Haishu Waterfront along the axes of cultural utility, primitive geometries, and formal expressions

Mapping studies of the patchwork ecologies that exist in and around the Haishu Waterfront district

Diagrams showing zones of extensive interchange between natural and artificial systems on the site of the Haishu Waterfront district

Developing a system of public and private architectural forms that enables an adaptive urban-planning strategy

Exploded axonometric connecting market-based scenarios for the phased construction of the Haishu Waterfront district

HAMILO PAVILION

PICO DE LORO, HAMILO COAST, PHILIPPINES

OUR DESIGN CONCEPT FOR HAMILO PAVILION WAS TO COMBINE A NUMBER OF PREEXISTING STRUCTURAL FEATURES WITH A CONTEMPORARY FAÇADE, MARRYING A SUBTLE SPACE WITH ITS EXTRAORDINARY NATURAL SURROUNDINGS. THE GLASS ENCLOSURE FRAMES PANORAMIC VIEWS OF PICO DE LORO BAY, FOCUSING OUR SIGHTS ONTO A NARROW HORIZONTAL BAND OF SPACE. THE DOUBLE-HEIGHT ROOF FOLDS OVER AN EXPANSIVE WOODEN TERRACE WITH A BLACK METAL MESH SURFACE, ESTABLISHING A PLACE TO REFLECT ON THE DIALOGUE BETWEEN NATURE AND MAN-MADE CONSTRUCTION. THIS 125-SQUARE-FOOT PAVILION PUNCTUATES A VERDANT FOREST WITHOUT OVERPOWERING IT. THE ROOF ACTS BOTH AS A SOURCE OF SHADE AND AS AN OPTICAL LENS FOR ITS VISITORS, REFLECTING THE SKY AND CREATING AN ILLUSION OF FLOATING OVER THE WATER BELOW. THE BUILDING HOSTS A RANGE OF SOCIAL EVENTS, WITH MULTIPLE POINTS OF ACCESS DEMONSTRATING THE STRUCTURE'S VERSATILITY AND ORGANIC POSITION WITHIN THE LANDSCAPE.

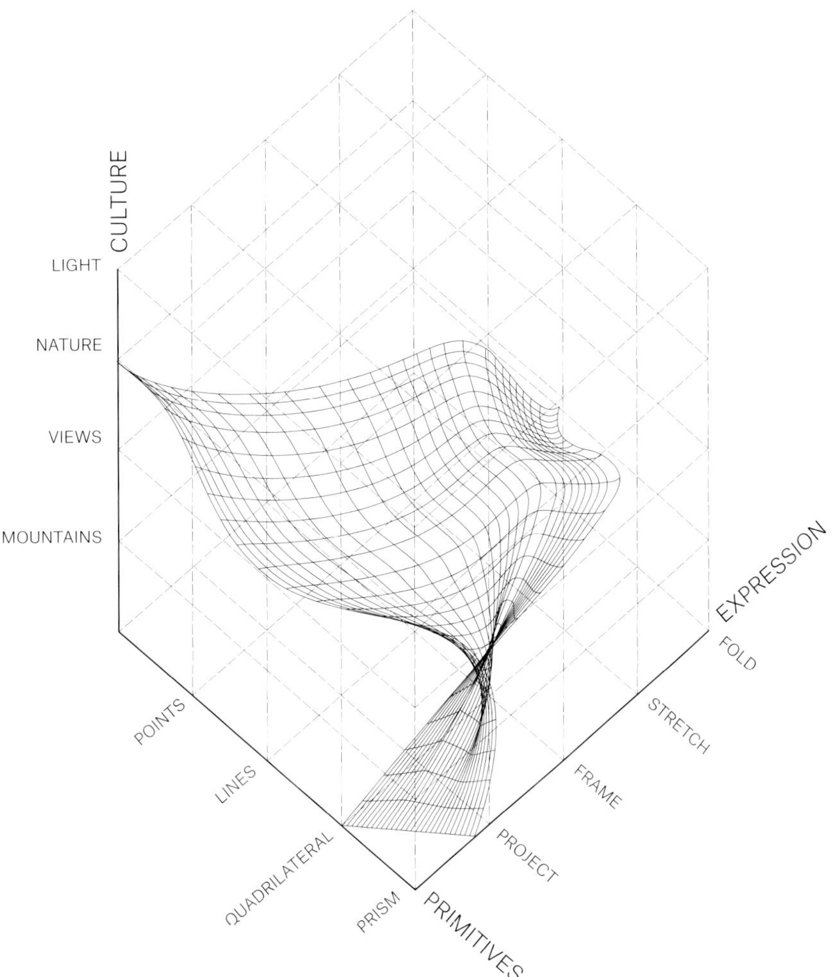

Plotting Hamilo Pavilion along the axes of cultural utility, primitive geometries, and formal expressions

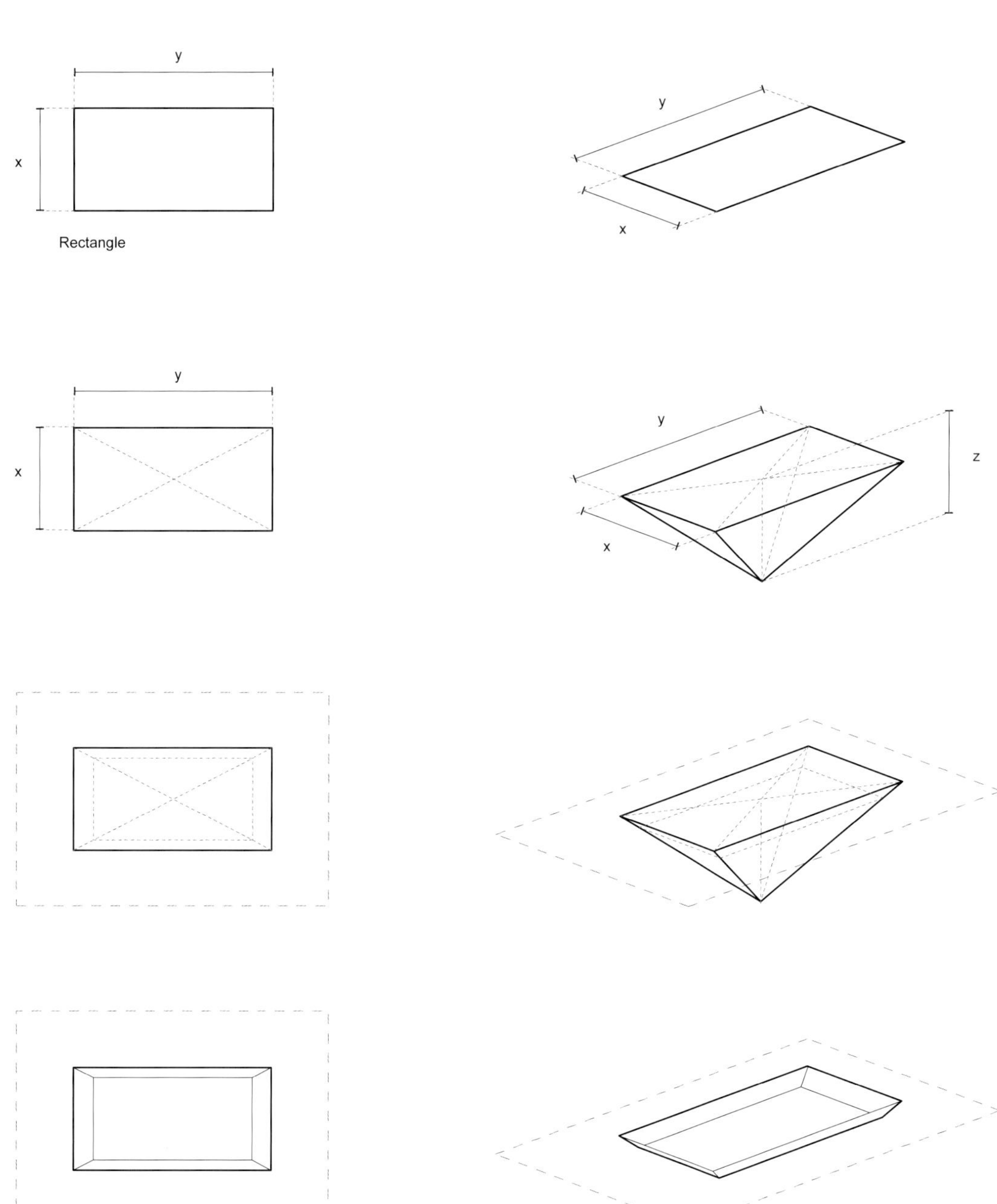

Studies into the creation of a viewing platform through
the intersection of a plane and a pyramid

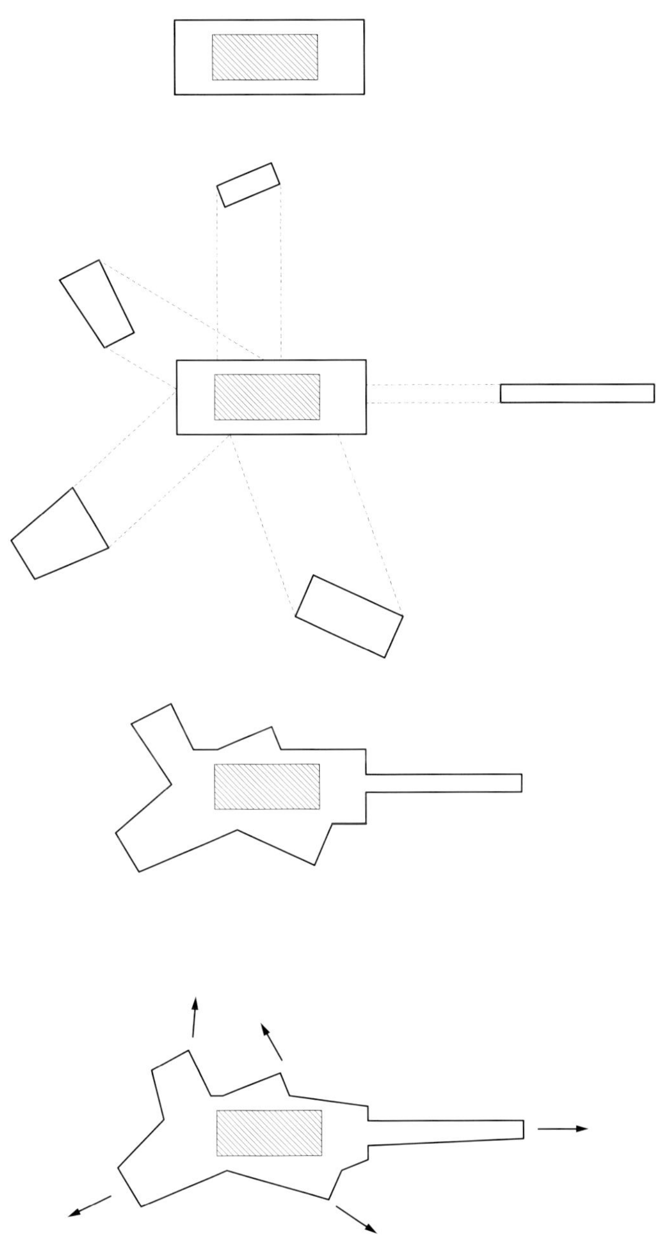

Diagram explaining the emergence of a multi-sided plan figure
with a primitive shape at its center

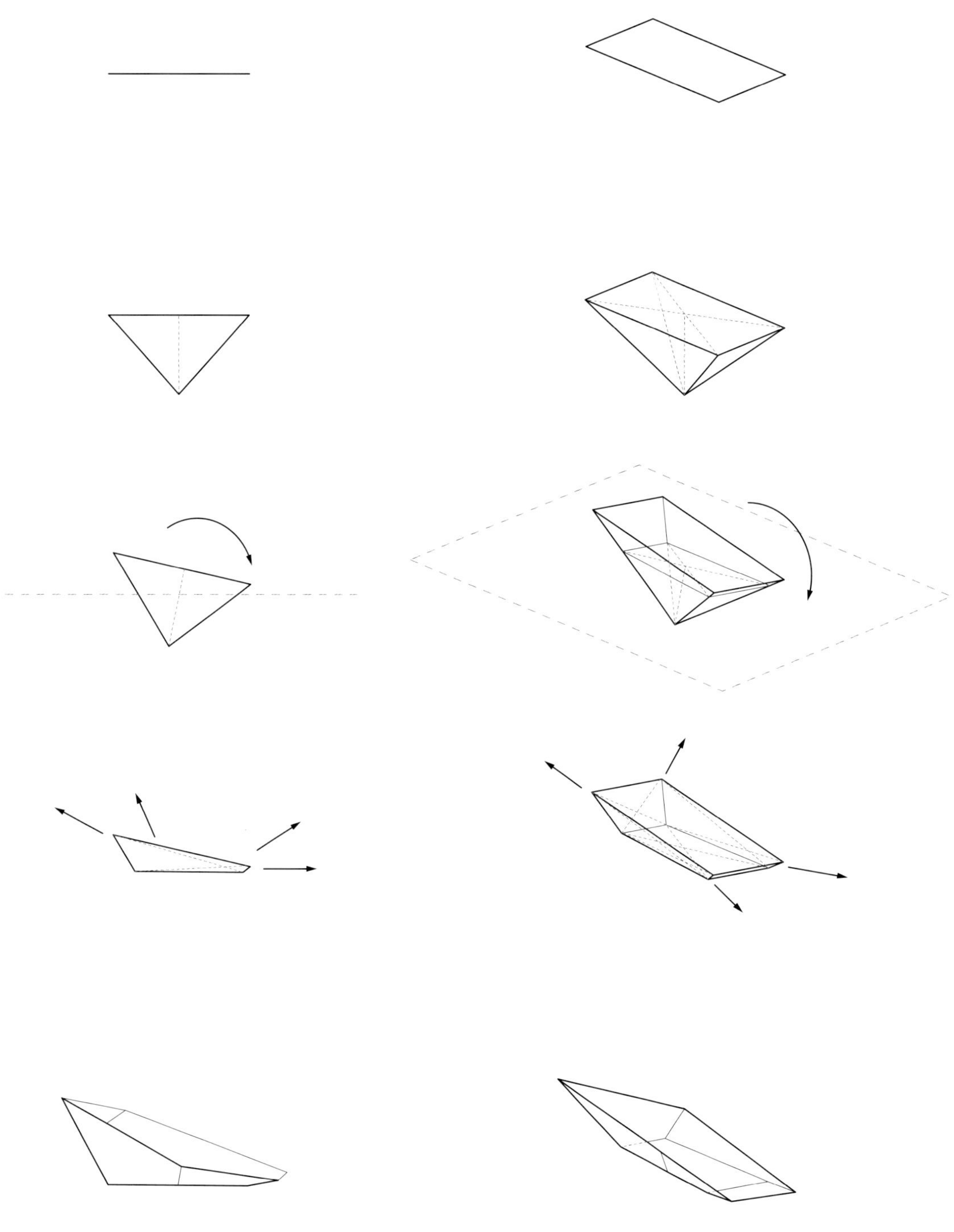

Developing a roof structure that enables one interior space to be the point of convergence for multiple exteriors

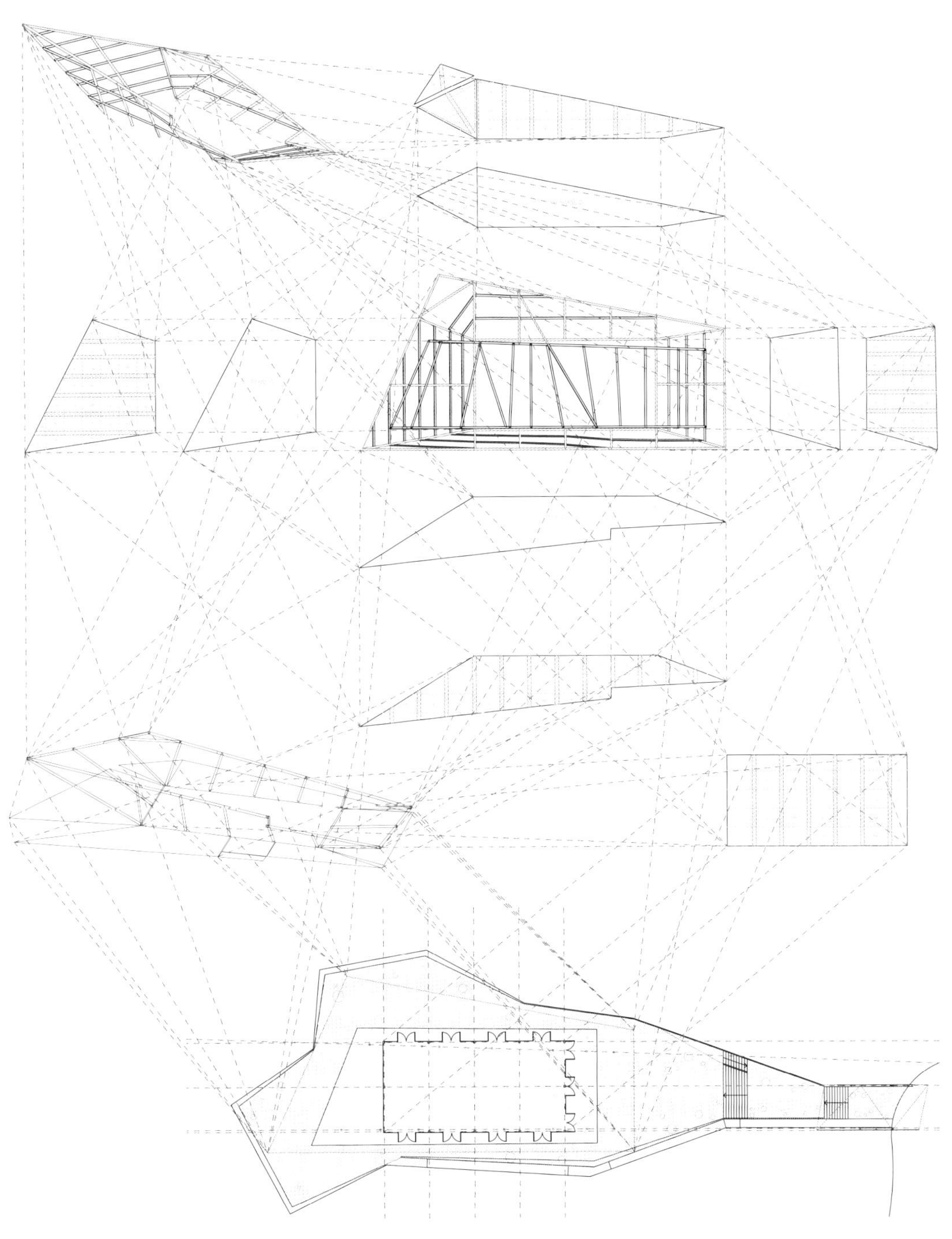

Exploded axonometric relating the roof structure, the ceiling canopy, and the view deck at Hamilo Pavilion

BALER HOSPITAL

BALER, PHILIPPINES

BALER HOSPITAL COMBINES THE FUNCTIONS OF A GENERAL HOSPITAL AND A TRAUMA CENTER AT A RURAL SCALE. OUR DESIGN IMAGINES BOTH A PRAGMATIC AND A FUTURISTIC SOLUTION TO THE CHALLENGE OF SUCH A SPECIALIZED AND EXACTING PROGRAM. THE LUSCIOUS EXTERIOR LANDSCAPE PERMEATES THE FACILITY THROUGH A SERIES OF UNDULATING CANOPIES THAT CREATES AN ARCHITECTURAL FIGURE IN AN OPEN FIELD OF GREEN. THE HOSPITAL'S PERIMETER PORTICO ACTS AS A STRONG ICONIC EDGE THAT HOLDS TOGETHER A VAST RANGE OF FUNCTIONAL DIFFERENCE WHILE STILL PRODUCING A SENSE OF LEGIBILITY FOR THE USER. THE GARDENS FILL THE HOSPITAL WITH AMPLE LIGHT AND GREENERY, CONNECTING PATIENTS AND STAFF WITH THE OUTSIDE IN A MULTITUDE OF WAYS.

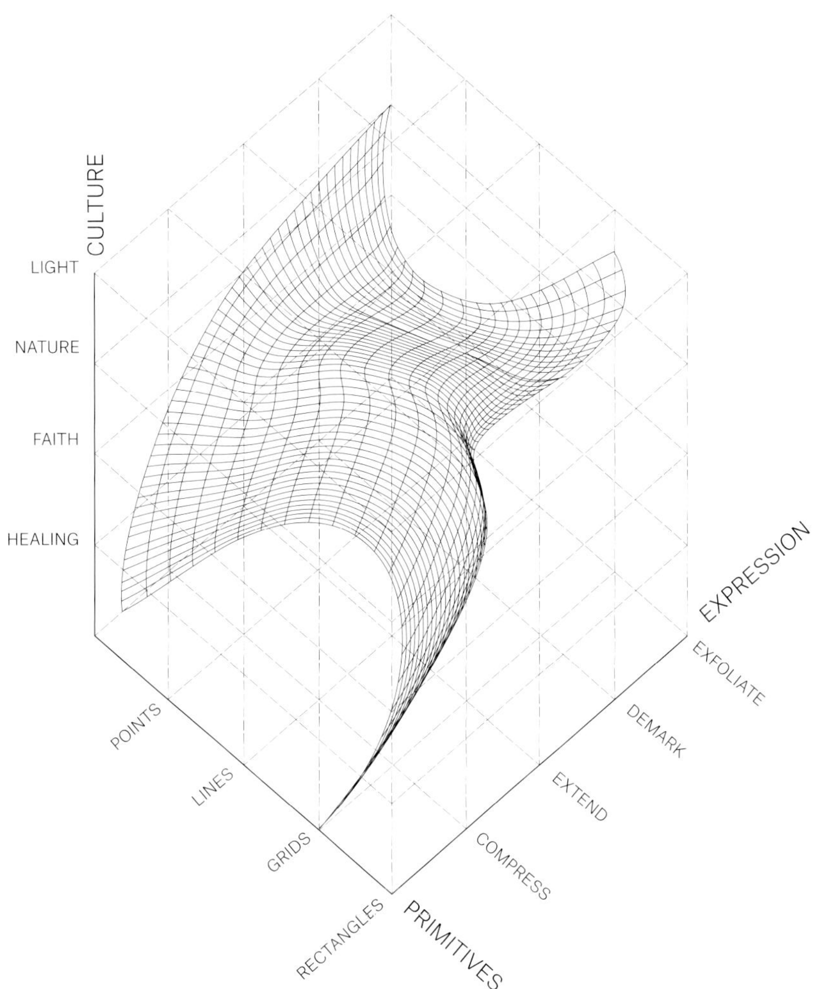

Plotting Baler Hospital along the axes of cultural utility, primitive geometries, and formal expressions

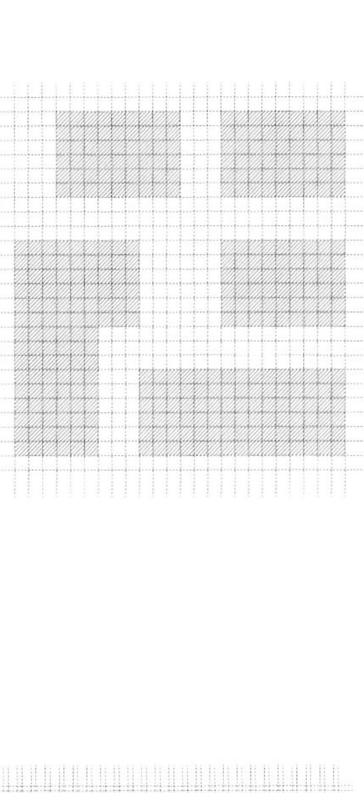

Grid studies exploring the synergies made possible by the combination of a general hospital and trauma center

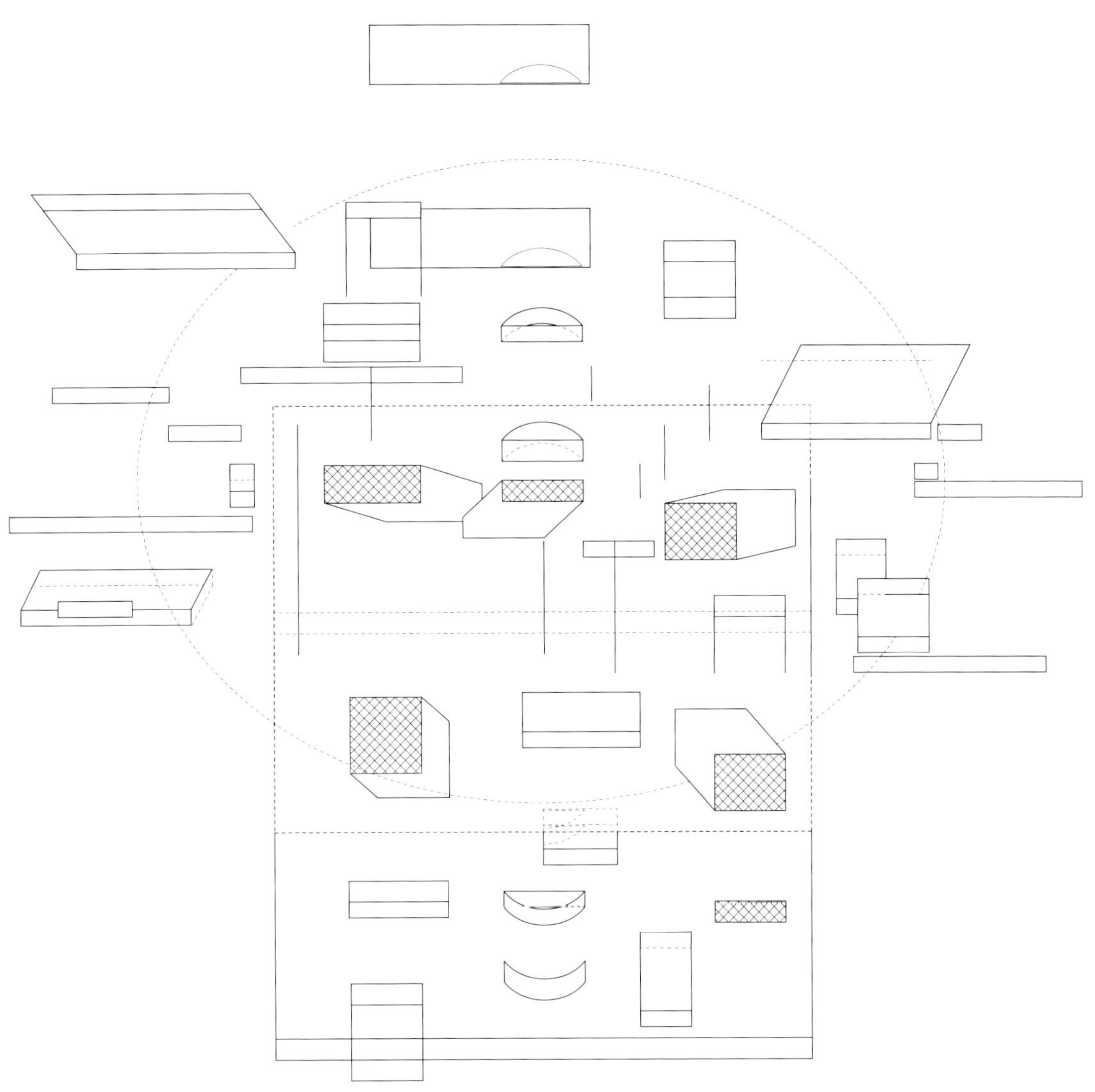

Diagrams modeling spatial connectivity of the Hospital's pocket gardens

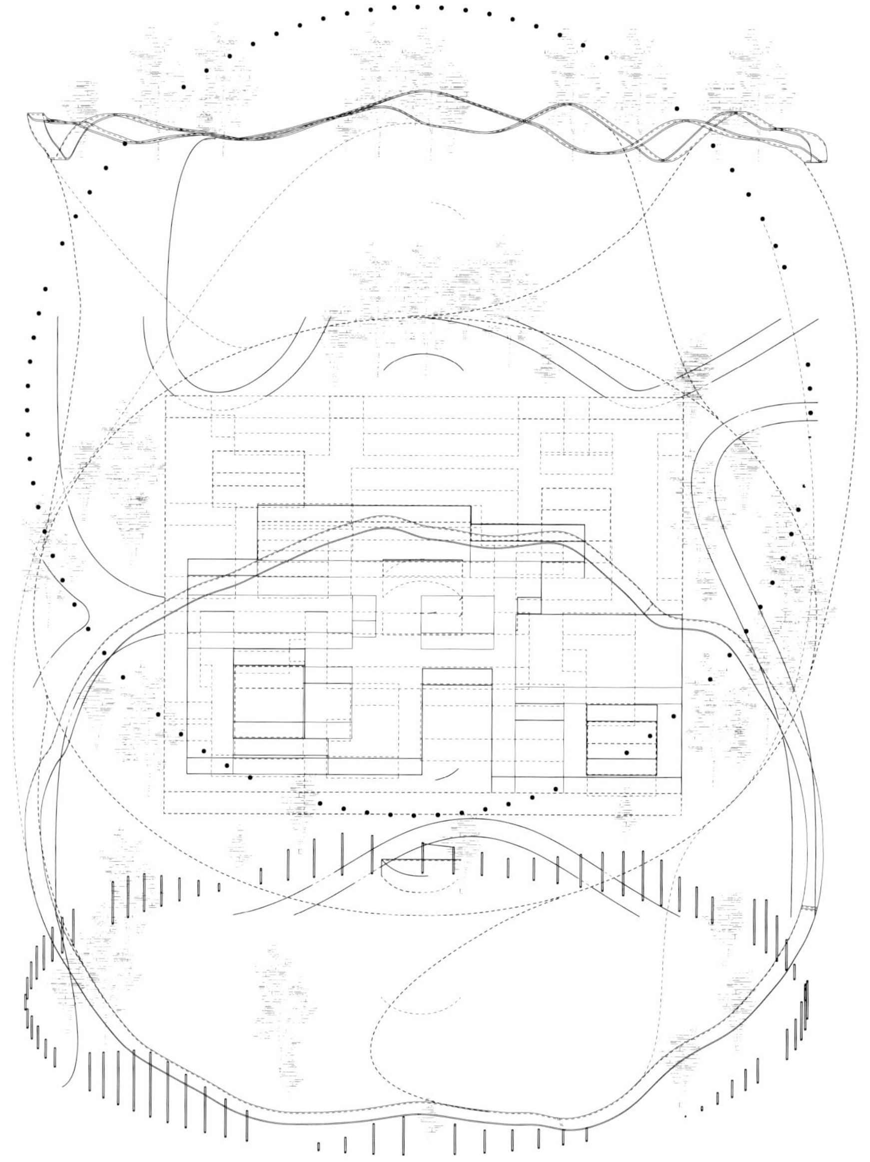

Bridging the confined world of hospitals and the lush tropical landscape
through a family of sinuous canopies

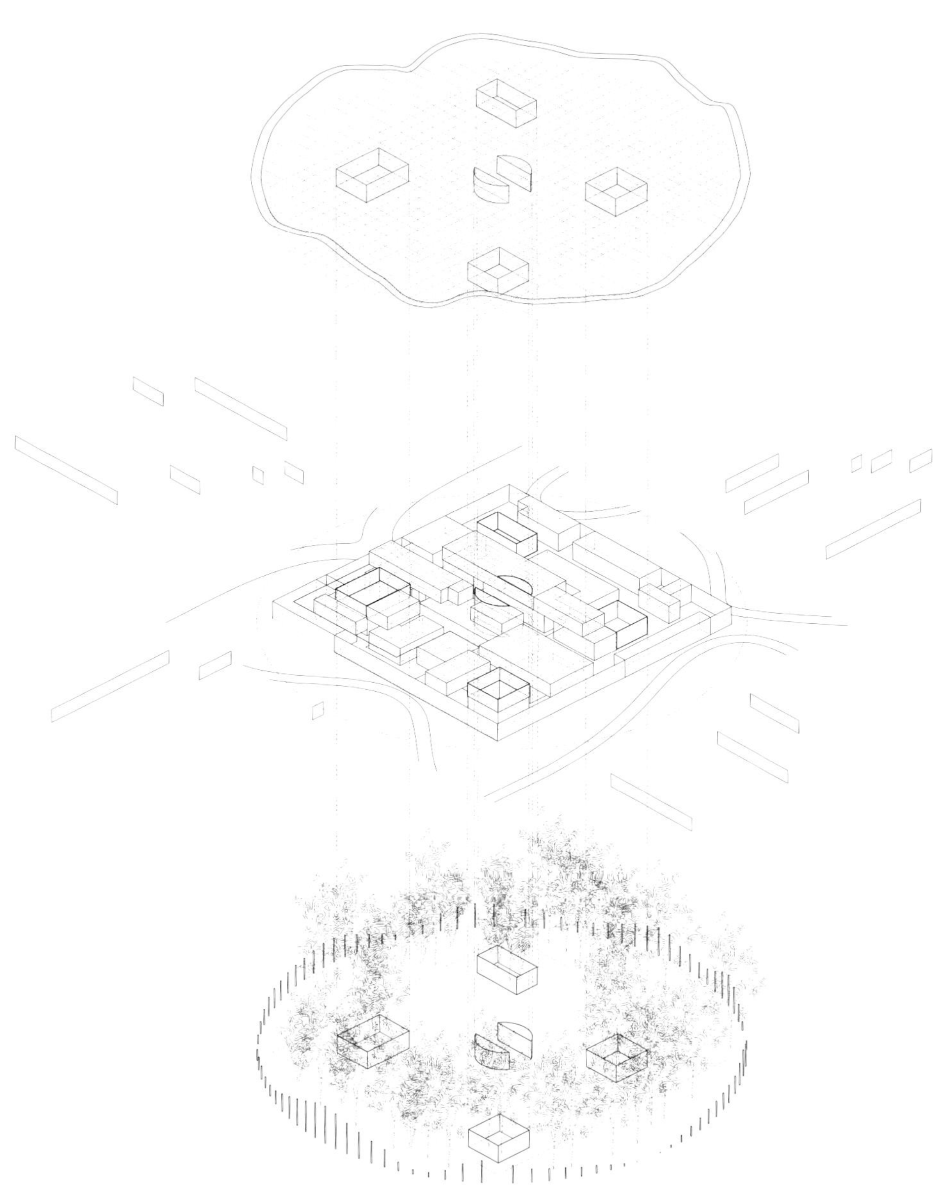

Exploded axonometric showing the relationships between the gardens, the patient rooms, and the canopies of Baler Hospital

LIO MARKET HALL

EL NIDO, PHILIPPINES

THE LIO MARKET HALL TAKES THE TRADITIONAL "IFUGAO" AESTHETIC OF THE SALAKOT HAT AND MULTIPLIES IT INTO A FIELD. THE RESULT IS A RECOGNIZABLE VISUAL PATTERN FOR THE TOWN THAT PROVIDES SHELTER FOR A SPECTRUM OF COMMUNITY EVENTS UNFOLDING BENEATH ITS ROOF. THE GROUND PLANE STITCHES TOGETHER THE COMMERCIAL STRIP AND THE NATURAL MANGROVE PARK THROUGH A LAYERING OF WOODEN HORIZONTAL SURFACES TO FACILITATE CIRCULATION AND THE CHANGING NEEDS OF MARKET-BASED OCCUPATION. THE MUTED TONE OF THE ROOF STRUCTURE DRAWS THE VIEWER'S ATTENTION BEYOND THE ARCHITECTURE TOWARD THE VIBRANT COLORS OF THE LANDSCAPE IT INHABITS.

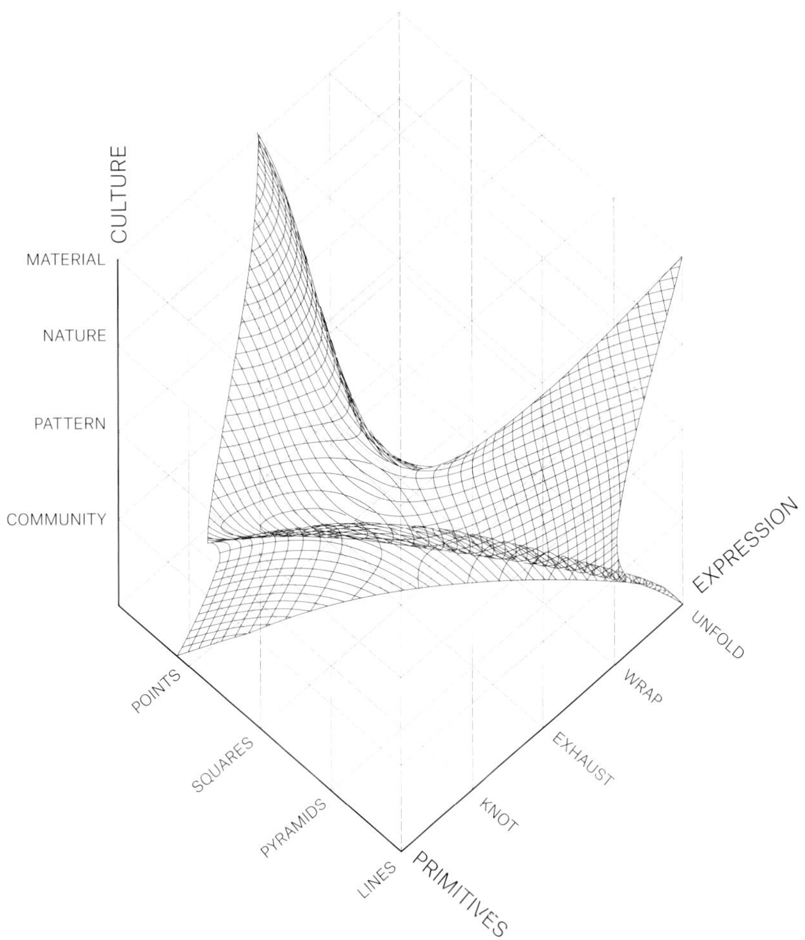

Plotting the Lio Market Hall along the axes of cultural utility, primitive geometries, and formal expressions

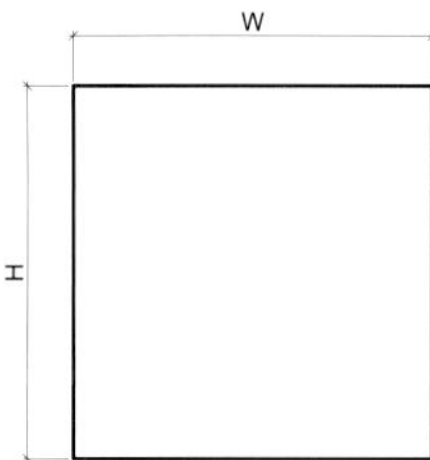

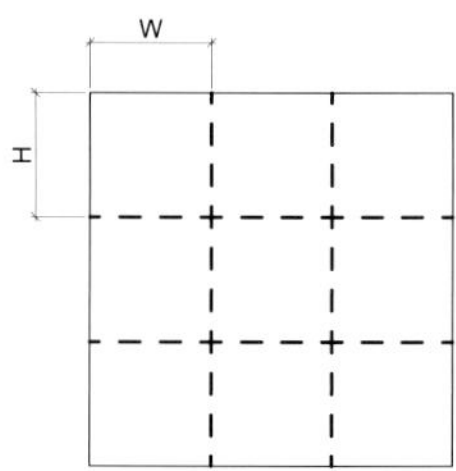

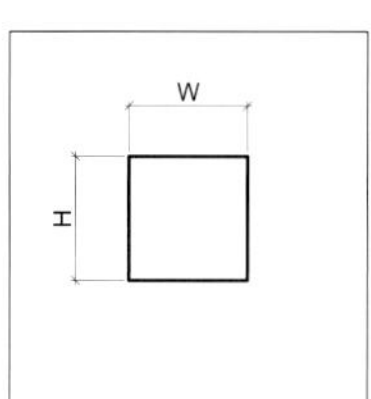

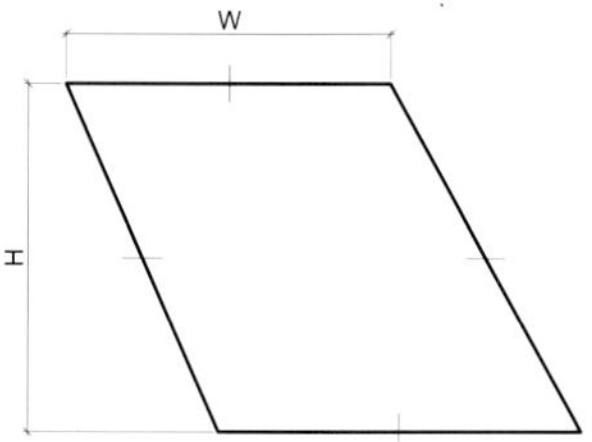

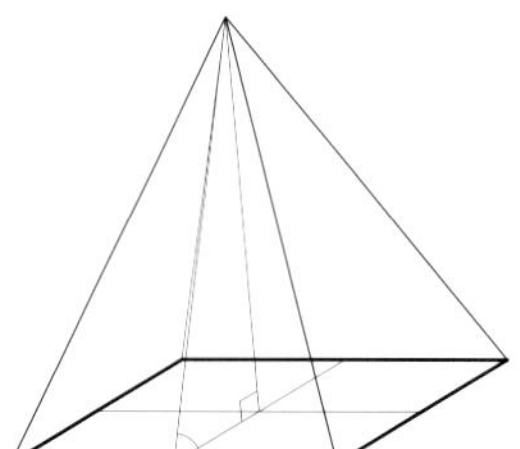

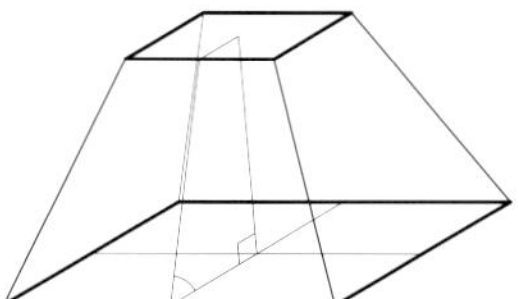

Studies exploring the potential of the salakot, a traditional Filipino hat, as an architectural form

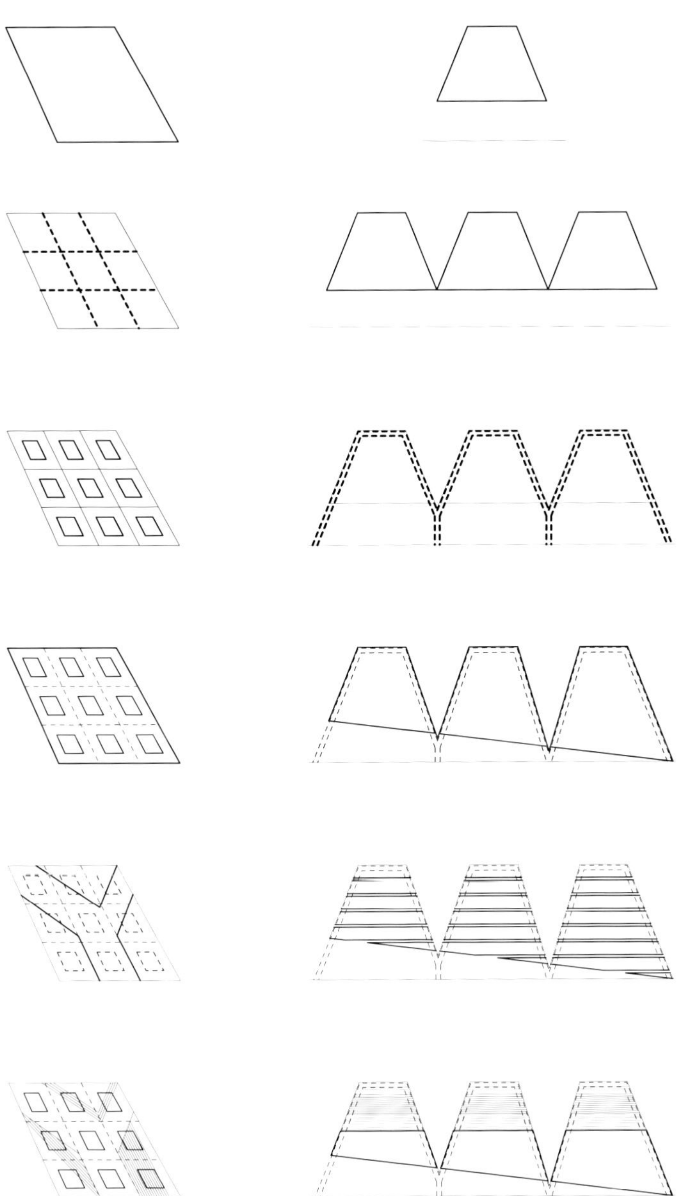

Diagrams showing the shifting relationship between the Market roof and the public platform

Considering the nine-square grid as an aggregation strategy for the Market roof

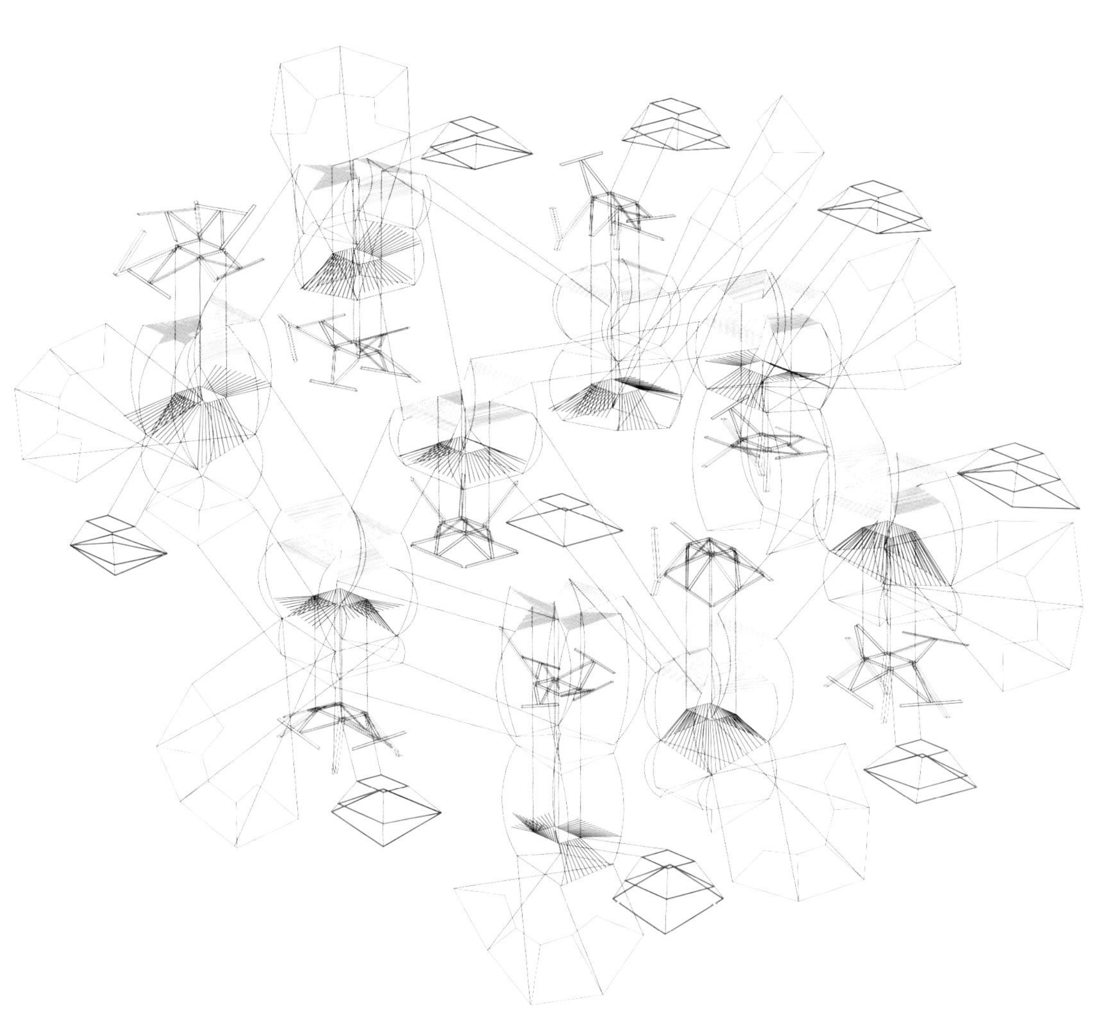

Exploded axonometric of the structure, skin, ventilation louvers, and public deck of the Lio Market Hall

TOWER ONE

MANILA, PHILIPPINES

THE HEADQUARTERS FOR ONE OF THE MOST DYNAMIC REAL ESTATE DEVELOPERS IN ASIA, TOWER ONE SITS A FEW BLOCKS FROM MANILA BAY, PHILIPPINES. THE STRUCTURE IS A SOLID MASS OF CONCRETE AND STEEL THAT ACTS AS BOTH A PUBLIC AND A PRIVATE SPACE, WITH VARIOUS RETAIL SPACES SEATED BELOW THE BUILDING'S SEQUESTERED UPPER-LEVEL OFFICES. THE BUILDING'S FAÇADE IS PUNCTUATED WITH A CASCADE OF PERFORATED CLEAR AND PURPLE-TINTED GLASS PANELS, ALLOWING LIGHT TO POUR INTO THE FIRST-FLOOR RETAIL AND PARKING LEVELS. AS THE BUILDING GETS TALLER, THE PLEATED ARRANGEMENT OF PERFORATED METAL PANELS TRANSITIONS INTO AN ICY PLANE OF CERAMIC FRITTED GLASS, PRODUCING THE APPEARANCE OF MOVEMENT AND LIGHTNESS THROUGHOUT THE EXTERIOR OF THIS SHIFTING CUBE-SHAPED CONSTRUCTION.

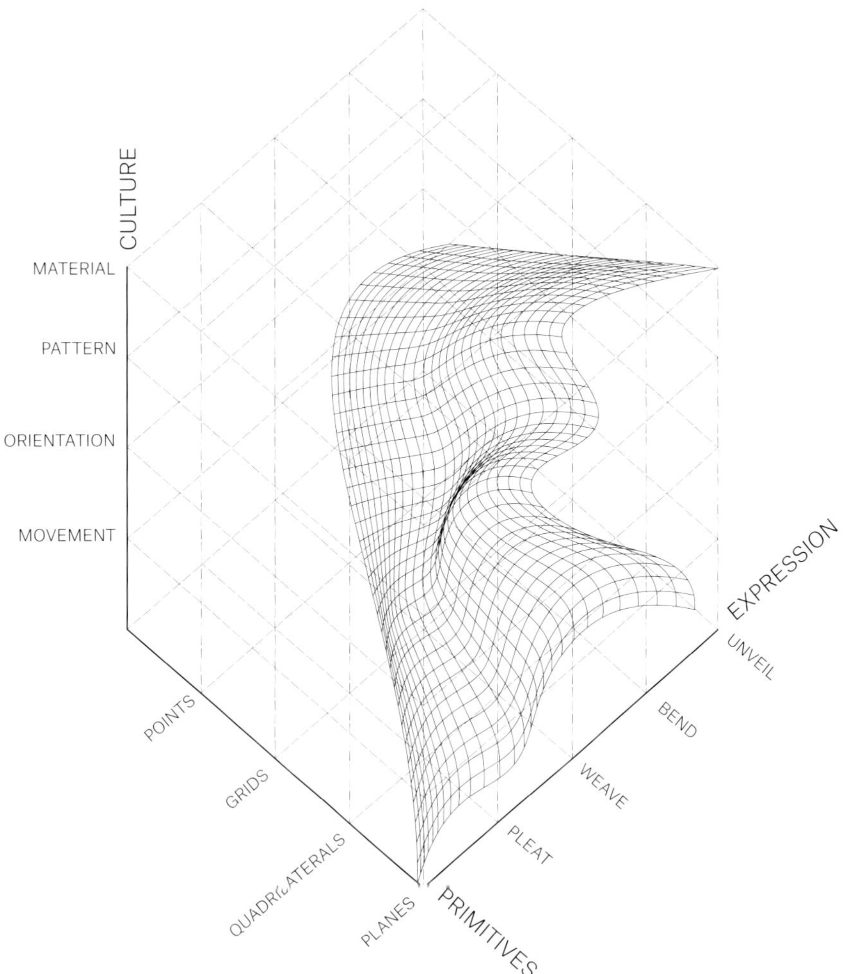

Plotting Tower One along the axes of cultural utility, primitive geometries, and formal expressions

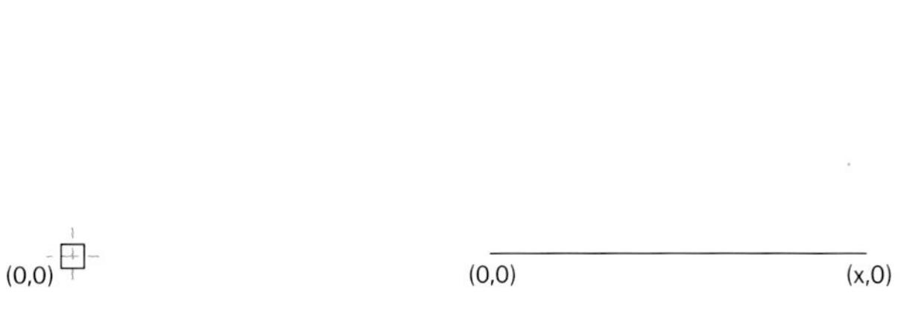

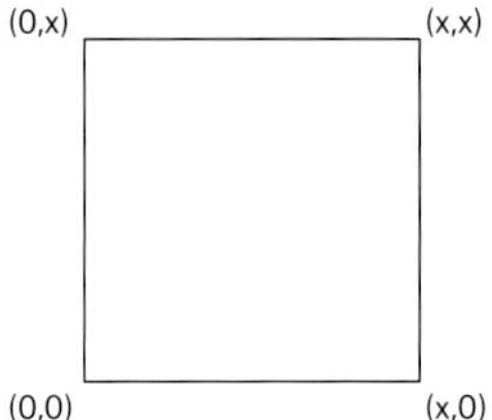

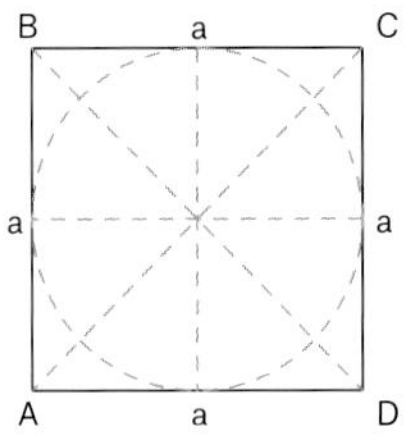

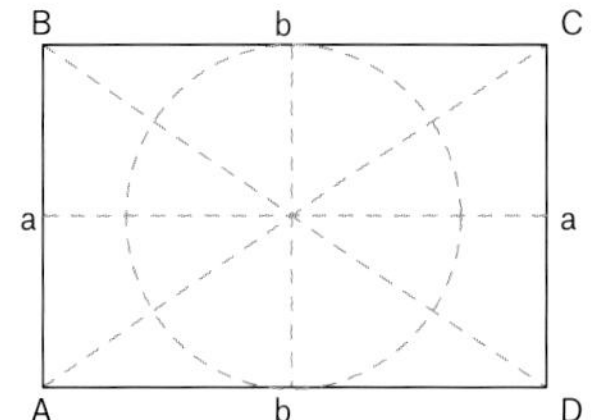

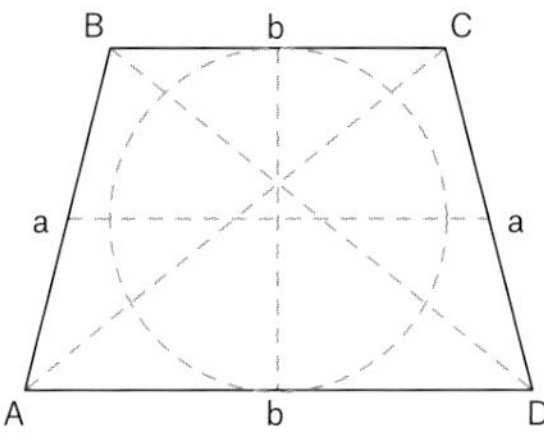

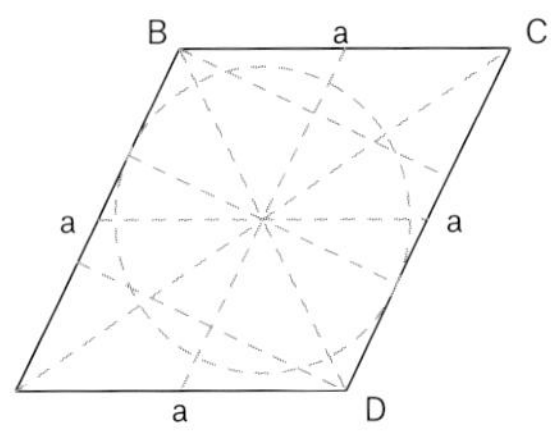

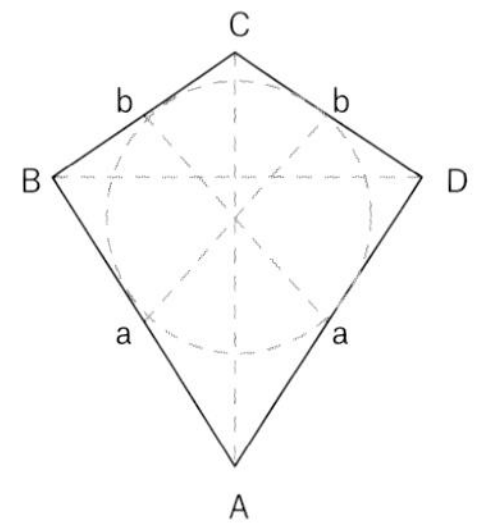

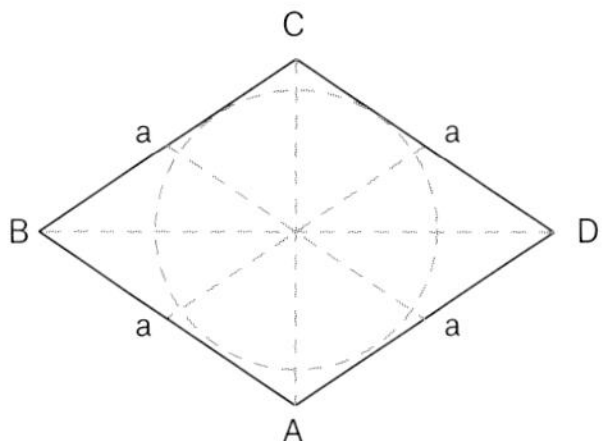

Studies into a four-sided diamond shape as an assembly of points around a circle

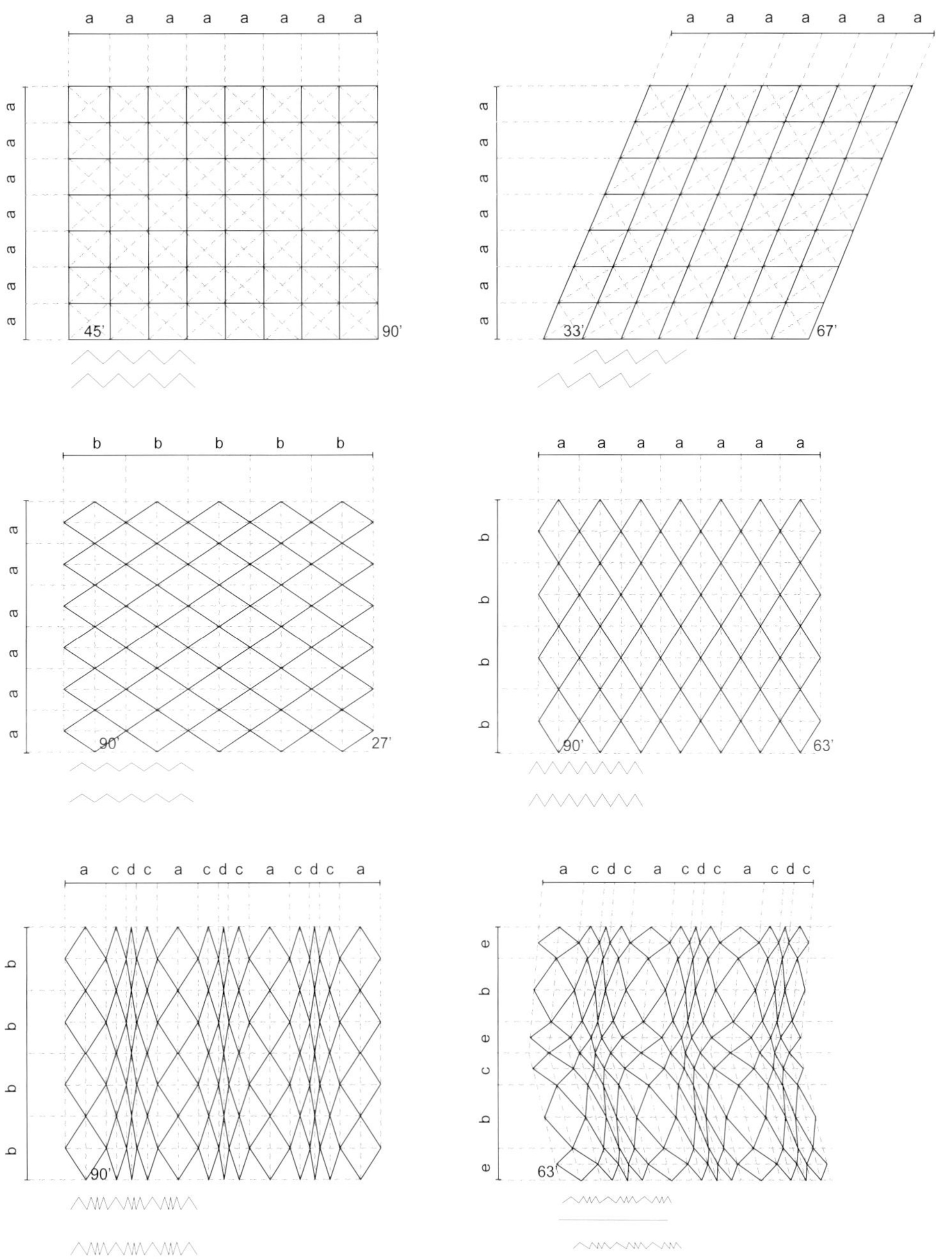

Tiling diagrams for the translation of a four-sided diamond into a building surface

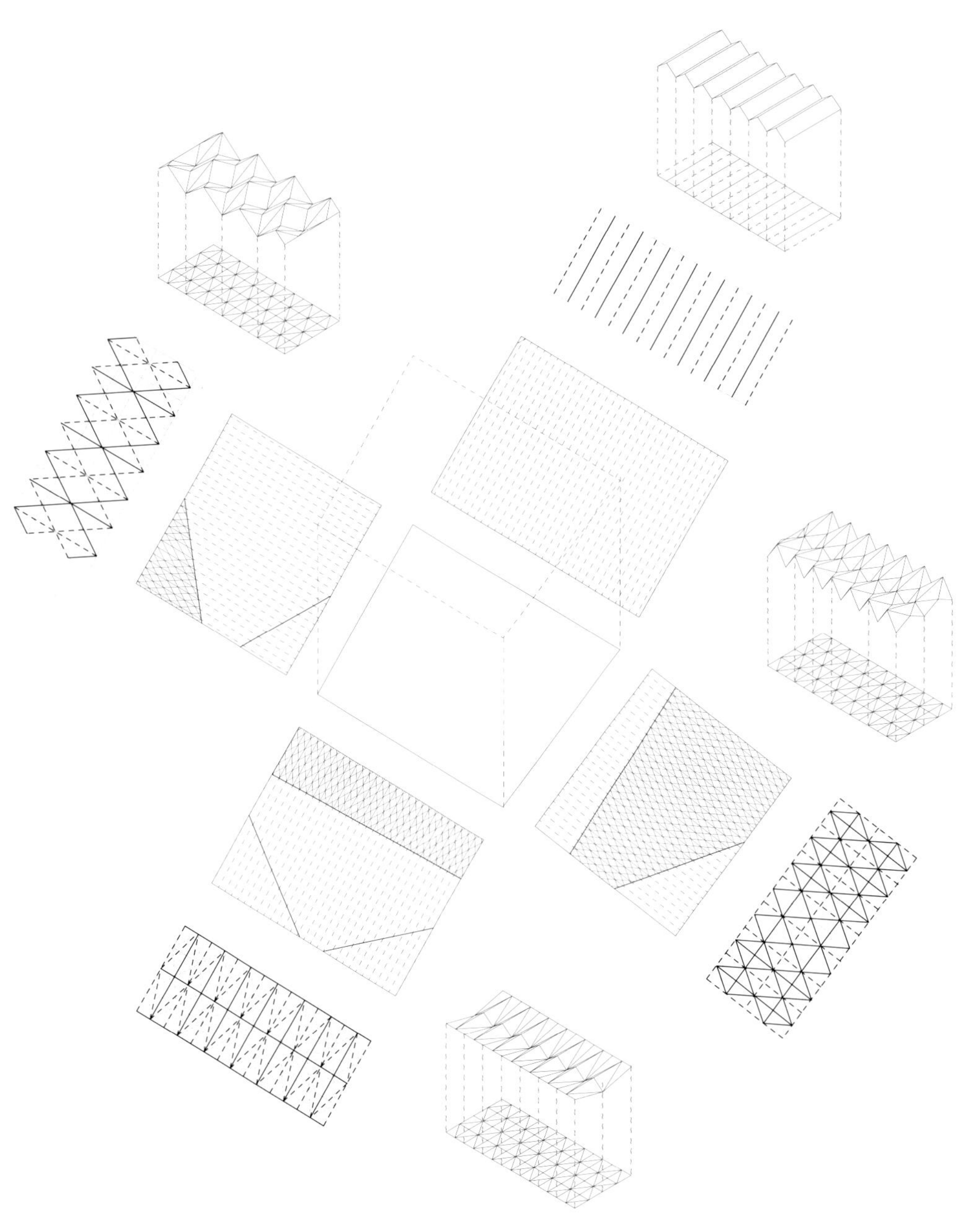

Creating volumetric differentiation across the surface of the Tower's façade

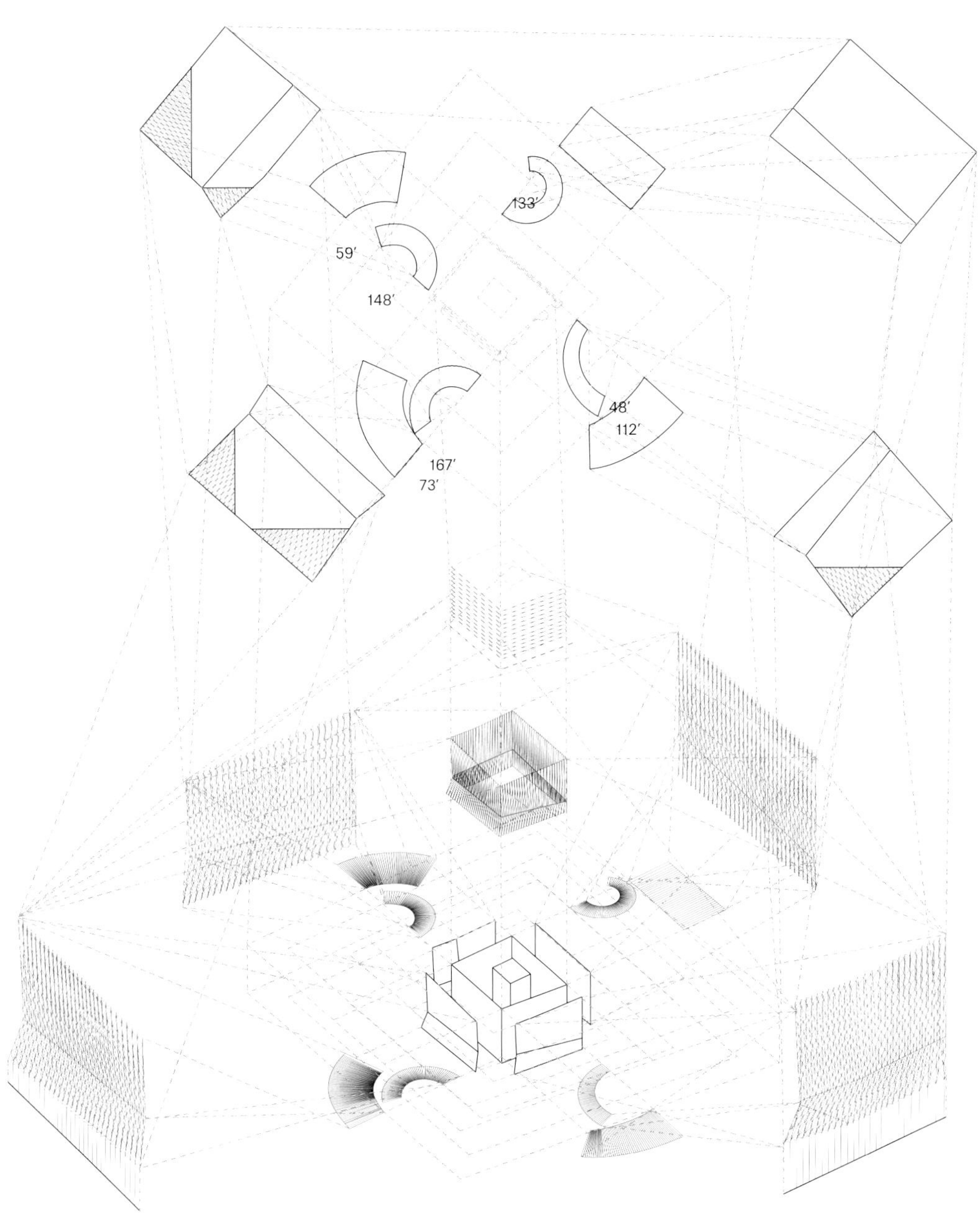

Exploded axonometric showing the way Tower One's façade
transitions from the smooth to the dynamic

PRADA

EVENT TENT

MANILA, PHILIPPINES

MANILA IS A COASTAL METROPOLIS OF 13 MILLION PEOPLE THAT HAS TURNED ITS BACK ON THE WATER. THE EVENT TENT ATTEMPTS TO REDRESS THE ABSENCE OF AN ACTIVE AND ACCESSIBLE URBAN WATERFRONT. THE STRUCTURE WORKS WITH TESSELLATED TRIANGULAR FORMS MAKING BOTH A FIELD AND AN ENCLOSURE. WE DESIGNED A HEXAGONAL ROOF UNIT OUT OF FOLDED STEEL PLATES, WITH ONE ASYMMETRICAL COLUMN THAT CAN BE ARRANGED INTO A NECKLACE WITH MANY CENTERS OF ACTIVITY. THE EVENT TENT RISES ON THE HORIZON WITH A SERIES OF UPTURNED HALF PYRAMIDS RESEMBLING A REGATTA OF PHILIPPINE SAILBOATS KNOWN AS *PARAWS*. THE PROJECT REPRESENTS THE IDEA THAT CONTEMPORARY CULTURE IS LOOKING NOT FOR SINGULAR MONUMENTS BUT FOR A SWARM OF INCALCULABLE IMAGES.

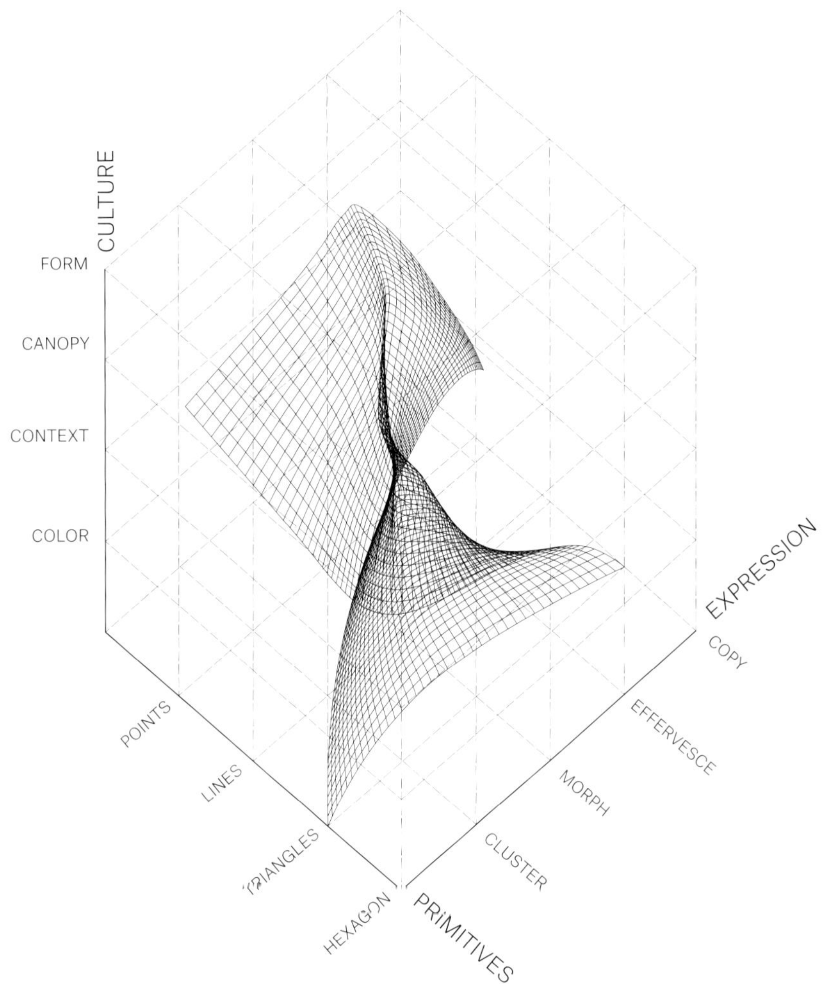

Plotting the Event Tent along the axes of cultural utility, primitive geometries, and formal expressions

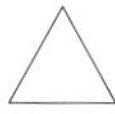
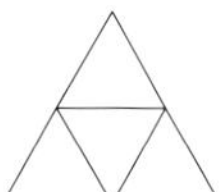
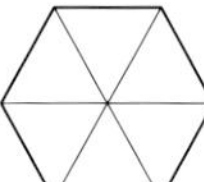
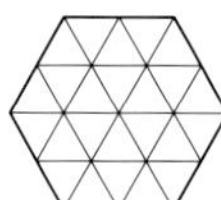
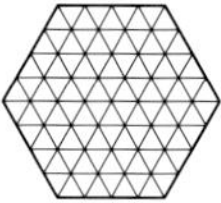
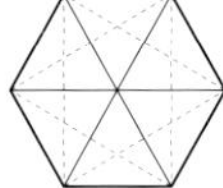

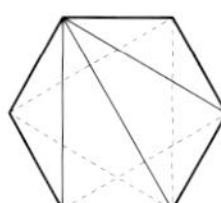
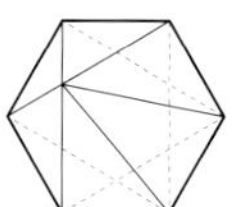
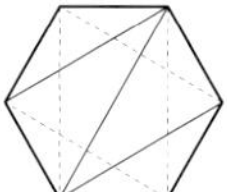
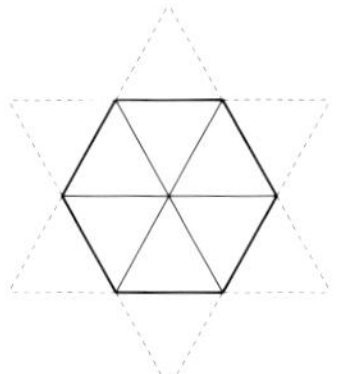
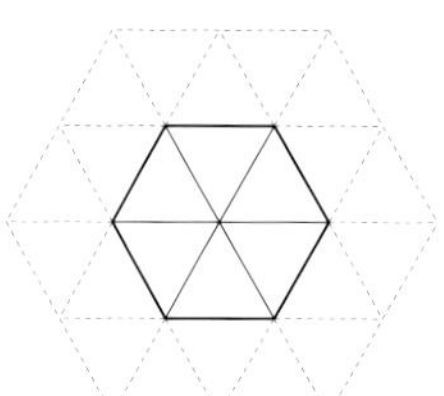
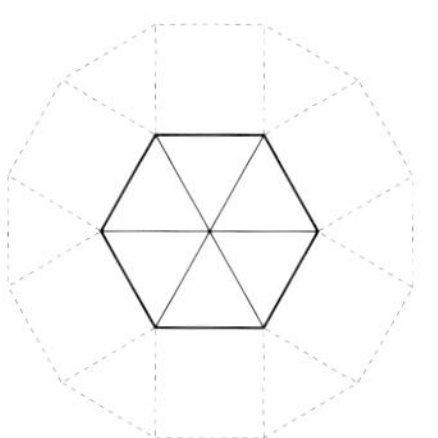

Tessellation studies into the development of hexagonal forms out of nested triangles

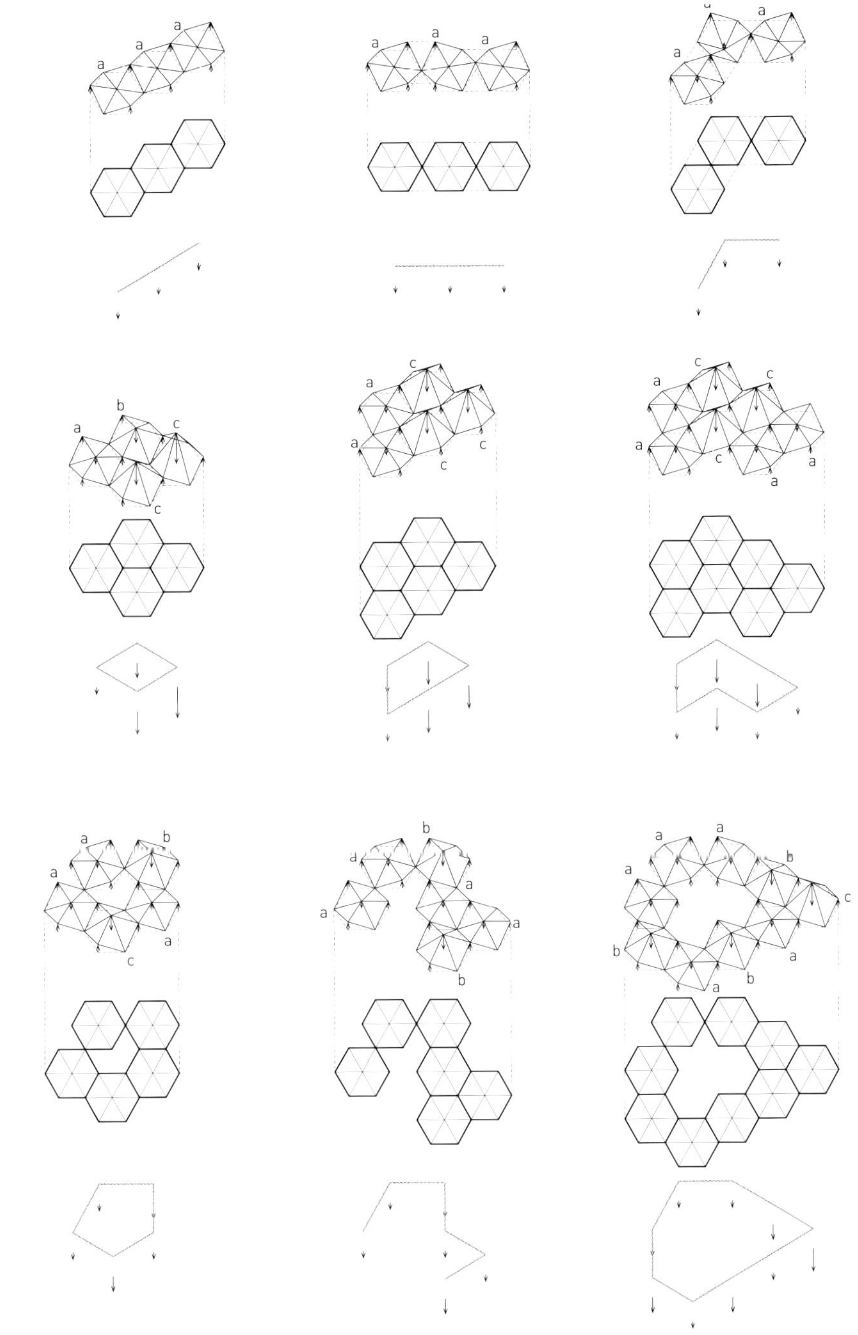

Tiling diagrams exploring different ways to produce open and closed event spaces

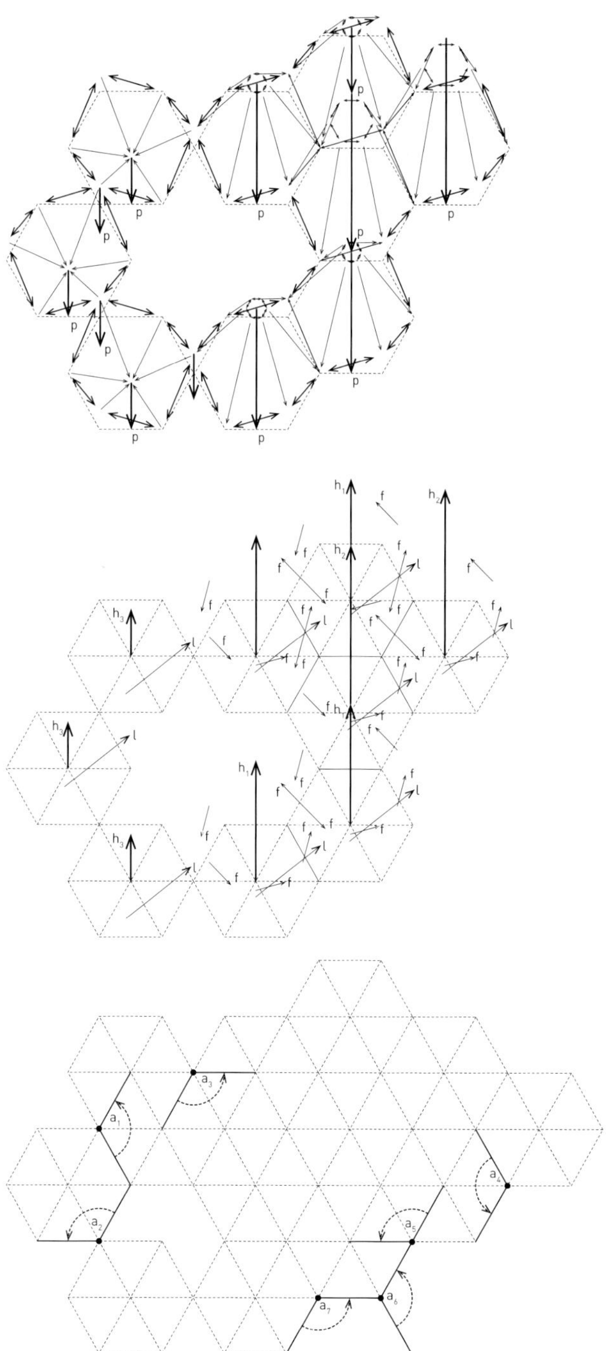

Creating a hexagonal layout that produces episodes of centrality while affording connections to the bay

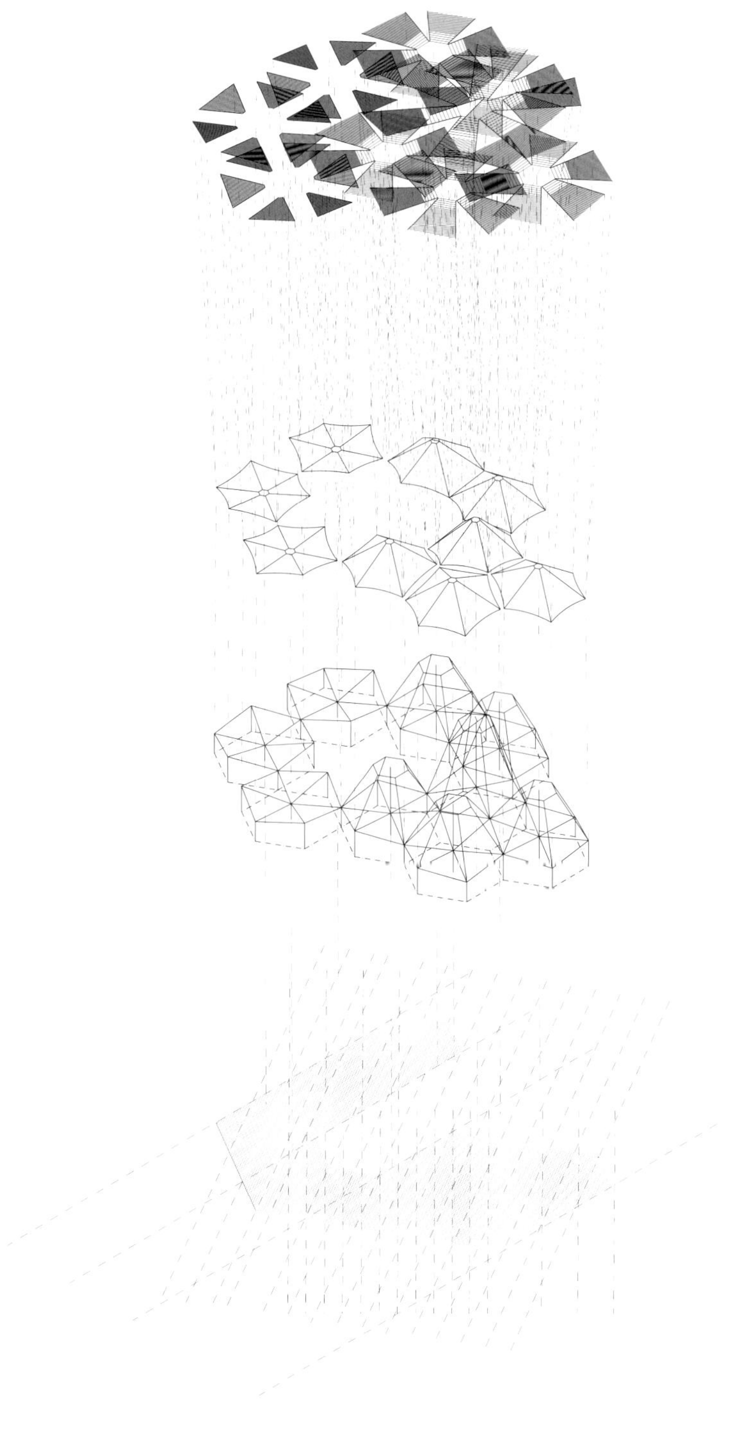

Exploded axonometric relating the folded plate structure with tensile fabric that makes up the Event Tent

FRAME HOUSE

PUNTA DE FUEGO, PHILIPPINES

THE FRAME HOUSE IS LOCATED ON A STEEP SLOPE OVERLOOKING THE SOUTH CHINA SEA. THE DESIGN CONSISTS OF A COMPACT ARRANGEMENT OF EQUALLY SIZED CONCRETE CUBES WITH ONE OUTWARD-FACING APERTURE. EACH CUBE DEFINES A DIFFERENT ROOM IN THE HOUSE, AND FRAMES A SPECIFIC VIEW OF OCEAN, SKY, OR GARDEN. THE EFFECT IS A HOME THAT IS CALCULATED YET WHIMSICAL, WITH A SERIES OF DISTINCT YET INTERCONNECTED ROOMS. THE ARCHITECTURE ENABLES A PLAYFULNESS TO EMERGE FROM A SELF-SIMILAR SYSTEM. THE FIRST-LEVEL CLUSTERS CENTER AROUND A SUNKEN GARDEN, THE SECOND LEVEL FOCUSES ATTENTION AROUND THE POOL, AND THE THIRD ORIENTS THE VIEWER OUT TOWARD THE WATERFRONT.

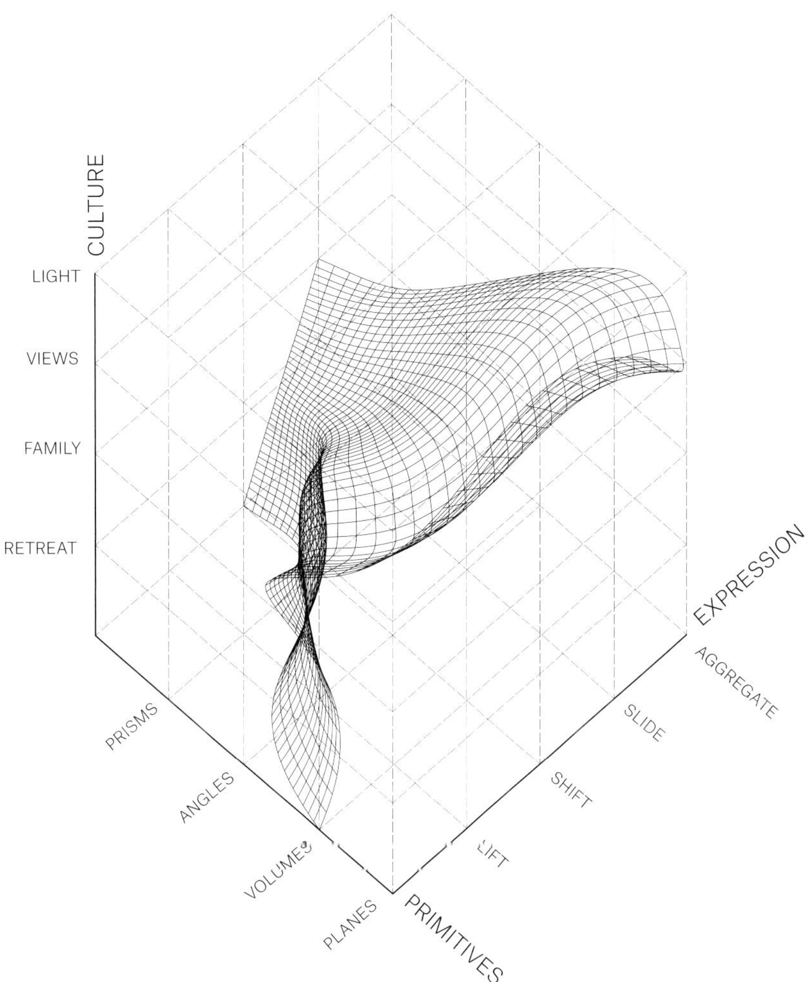

Plotting the Frame House along the axes of cultural utility, primitive geometries, and formal expressions

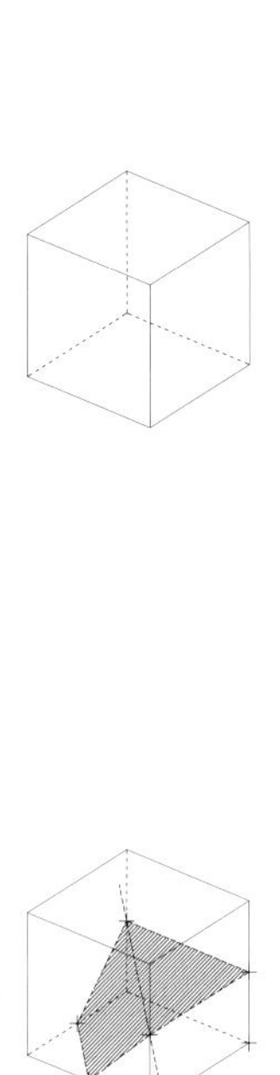
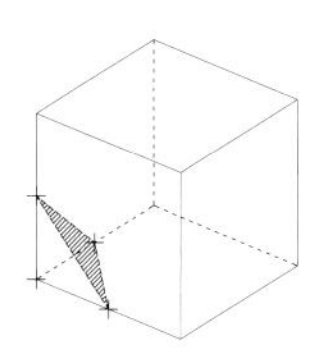
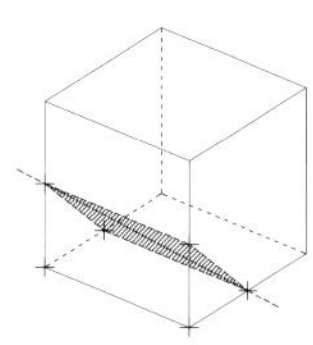
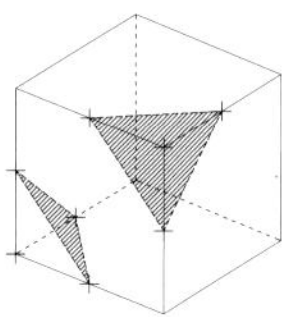
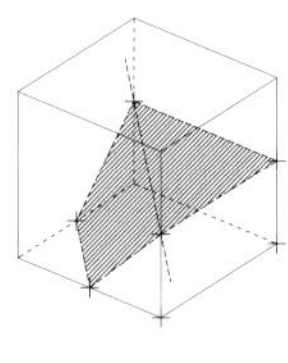
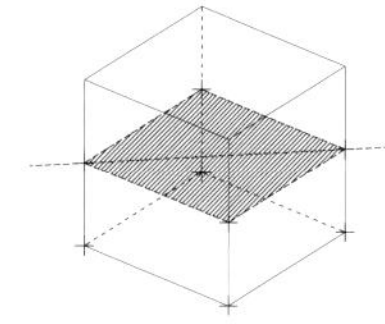
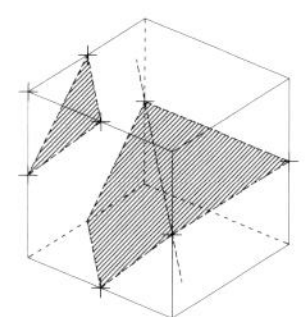
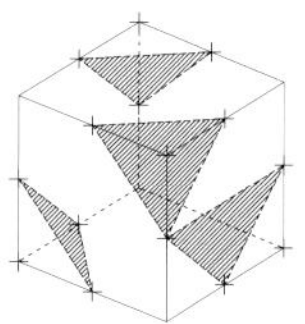
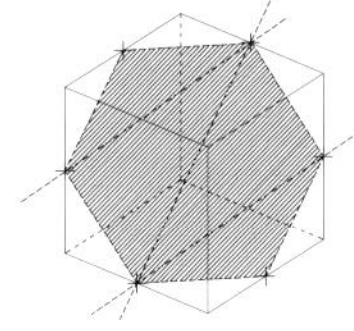
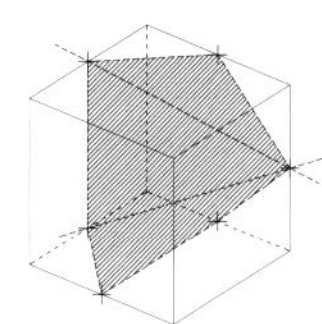
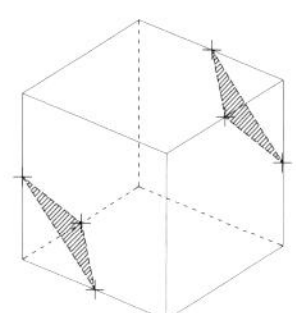
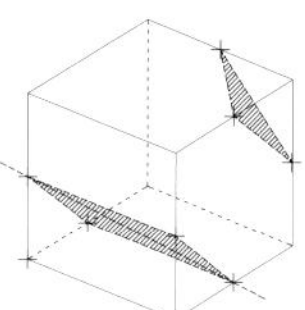
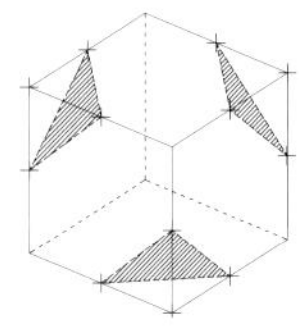
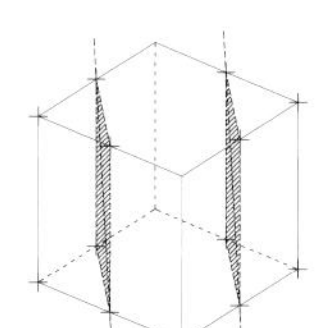
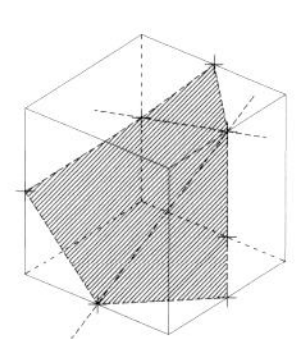
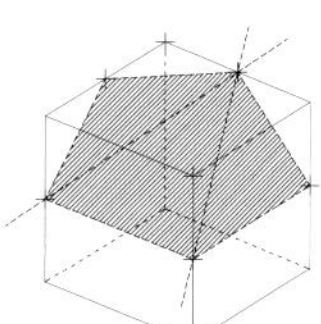

Studies into the ways of opening a cube with intersecting planes

Unfolded diagrams describing how a cube becomes a room with a view

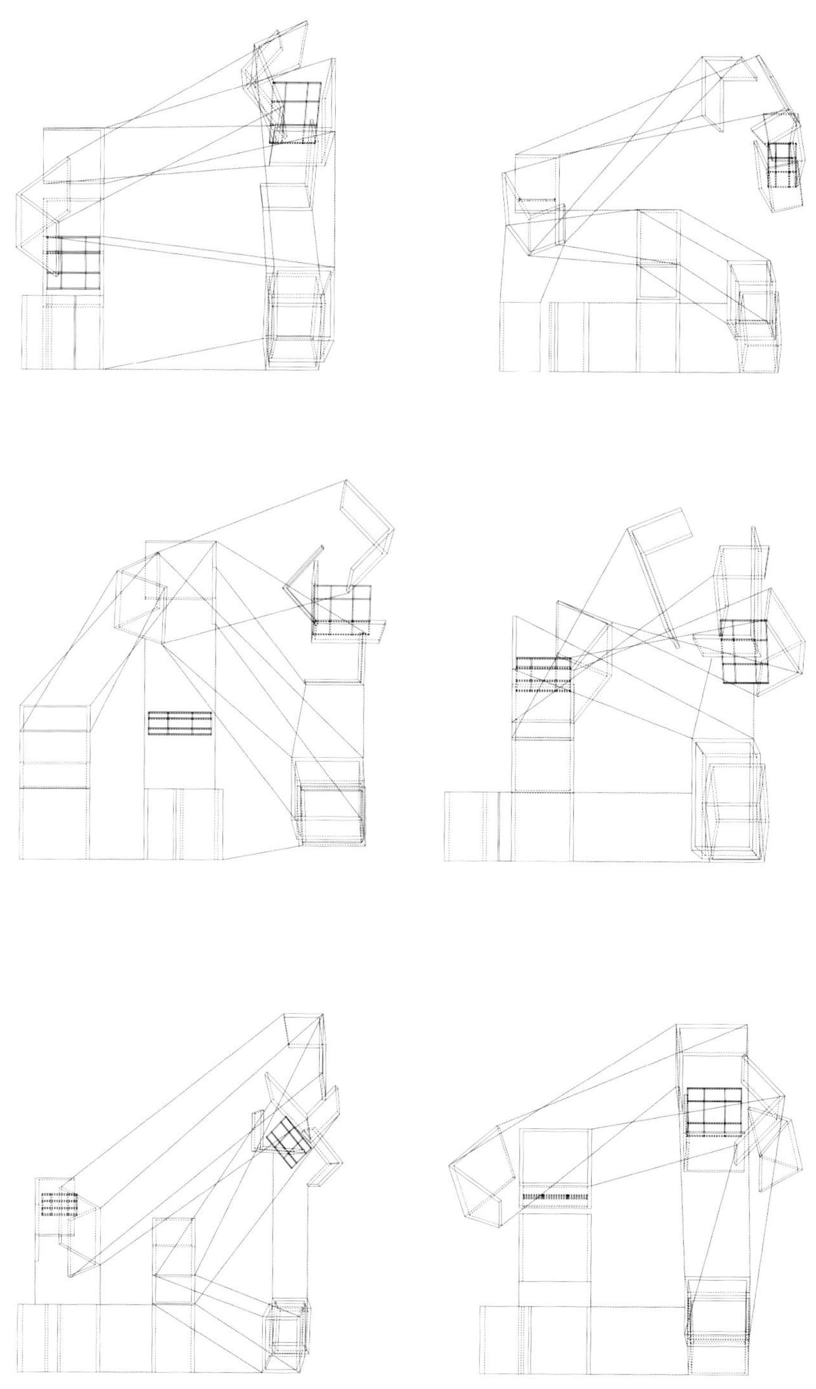

Creating domesticity through an aggregation of rooms that frame the landscape

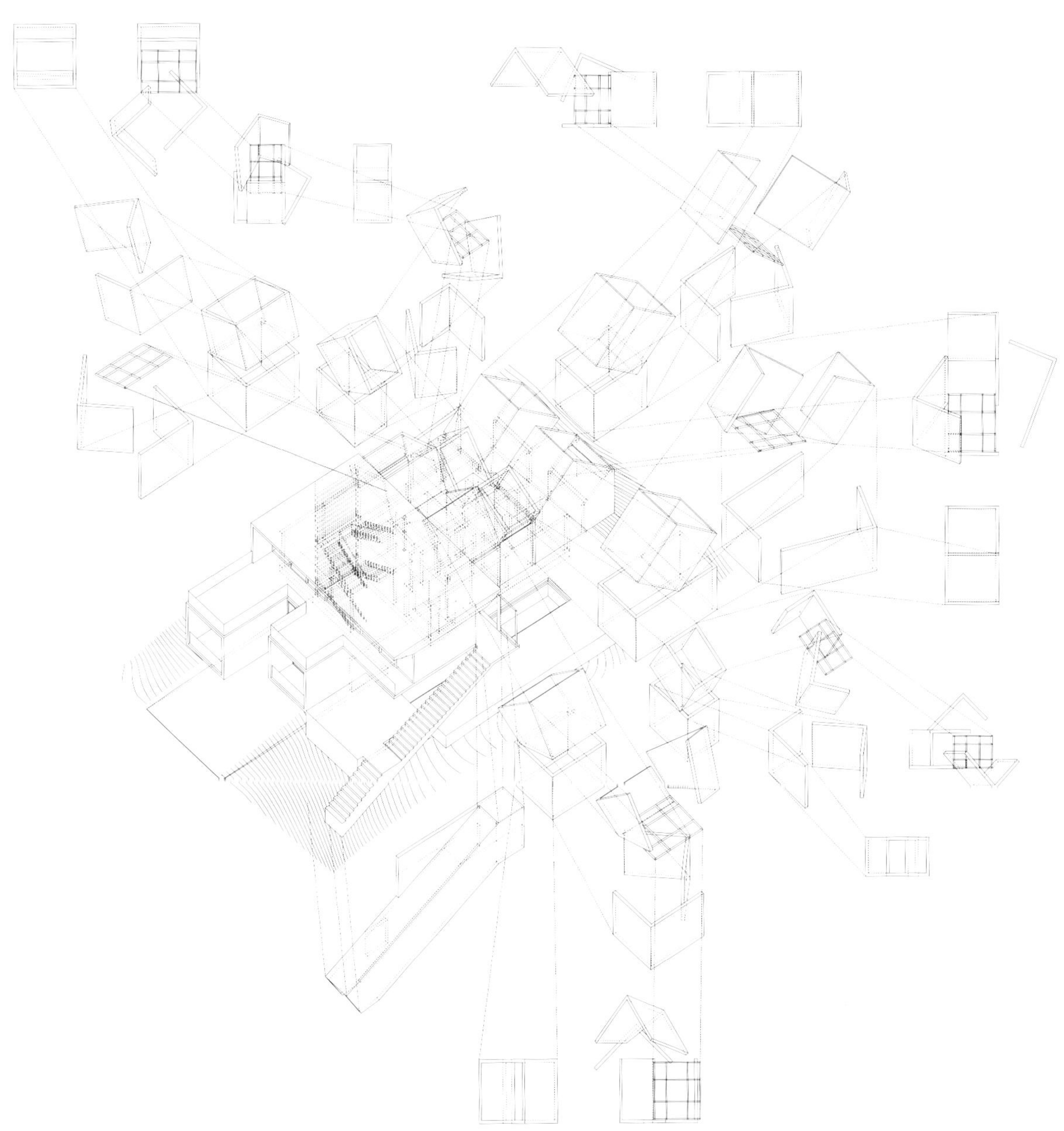

Exploded axonometric relating each cube with the frames that make the Frame House

LA SALLE CHURCH

BIÑAN CITY, PHILIPPINES

THE DESIGN OF THE CHURCH PLAYS WITH THE IDEA OF BOUNDARIES, BETWEEN THE LIGHTNESS OF THE POROUS SKIN AND THE WEIGHT OF THE SANCTUARY. HOW DO WE GO FROM BEING OUTSIDE OF A GROUP TO BEING WITHIN A FAITH? THROUGH AN ARRAY OF TANGENT CIRCLES, THE CHURCH CREATES POCKETS FOR LITURGICAL FUNCTIONS THAT VARY IN SPATIAL CONSTRAINTS AND DEGREES OF FORMALITY, PLACING US ALONG THE PERIPHERY OF A SPACE IN ORDER TO REVEAL INSIDE AND OUTSIDE AS CONTINGENT STATES OF BEING. AS PART OF A LARGER UNIVERSITY MASTER PLAN, THE CHURCH IS AN INTEGRAL COMPONENT IN WEAVING TOGETHER CULTURE AND ECOLOGY BY OFFERING USERS A DIFFERENT IDEA OF INCLUSIVENESS.

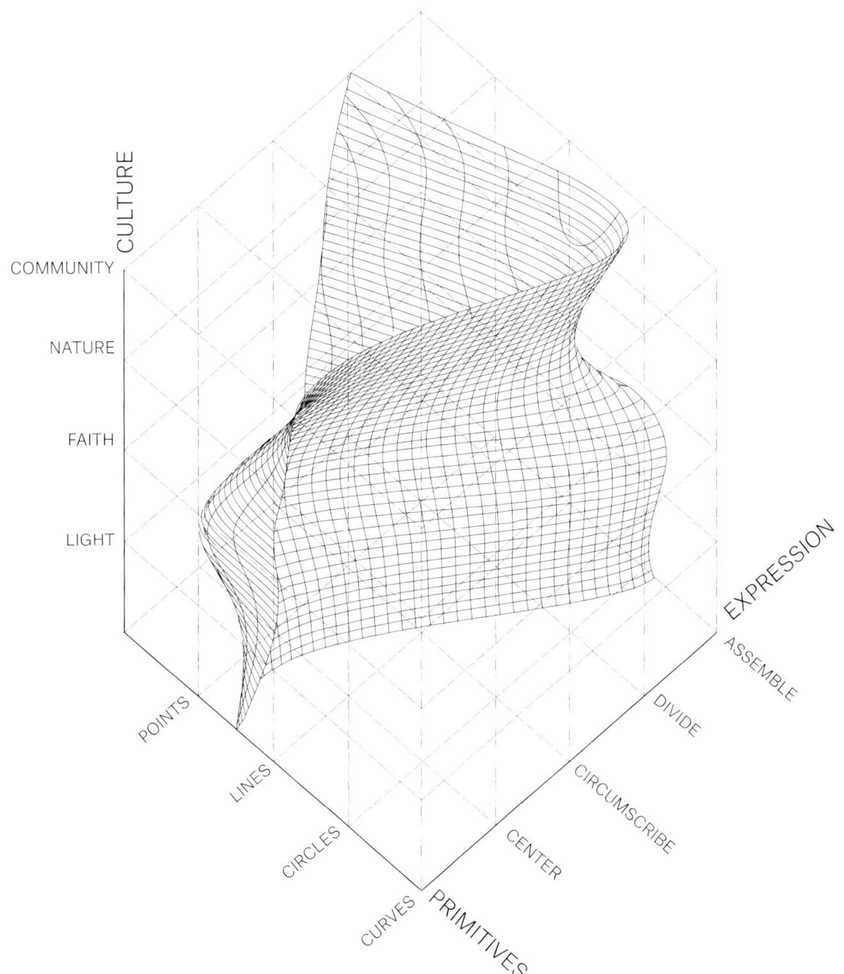

Plotting La Salle Church along the axes of cultural utility, primitive geometries, and formal expressions

Studies into aggregating forms with a shared center

Diagrams showing the genesis of auxiliary spaces in the Church

Mapping the gardens and pathways surrounding the Church

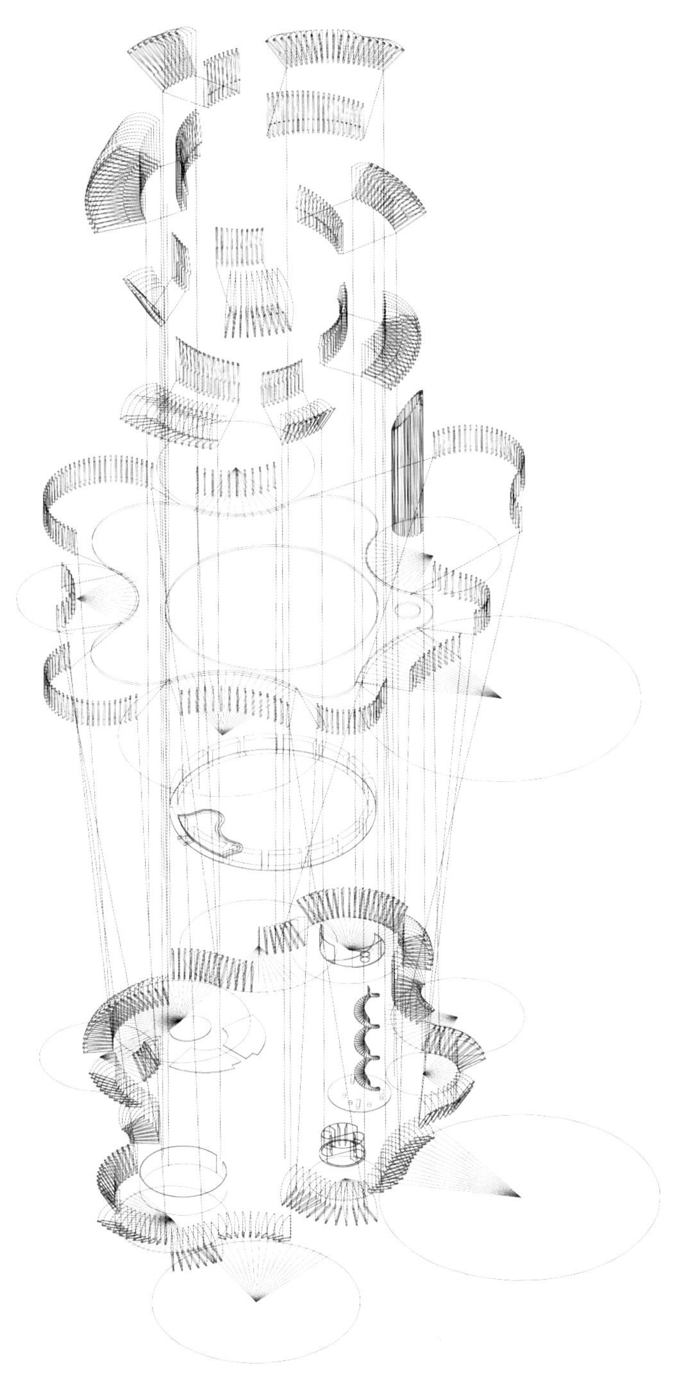

Exploded axonometric showing radiating columns as they define the congregational interior, surrounded by the star-shaped loggia in La Salle Church

BOGOTÁ CENTRO

BOGOTÁ, COLOMBIA

THE LARGEST SINGLE URBAN INTERVENTION TO DATE IN BOGOTÁ, THIS MASTER PLAN HAS THE POTENTIAL TO REIMAGINE THE WAY BOGOTANOS RELATE TO THEIR CITY. THE 72-HECTARE SITE REVISITS THE IDEA OF COMPACTNESS AND DIVERSITY IN THE CITY THROUGH THE CREATION OF DISTRICTS WITHIN A NETWORK OF INTERMEDIATE PUBLIC PARKS, EACH WITH ITS OWN FAMILY OF MIXED-USED BUILDINGS THAT IN TURN DEFINE SHARED PRIVATE OPEN SPACES. INFORMED BY TYPOLOGICAL RESEARCH INTO EXISTING FORMS OF COLLECTIVE HOUSING IN COLOMBIA AND AN ANALYSIS OF THE STREET GRIDS OF THE SURROUNDING NEIGHBORHOODS, THE MASTER PLAN PROPOSES A FRAMEWORK FOR ACTION. THE DESIGN ACKNOWLEDGES THE REALITY OF BOGOTÁ AS A SHIFTING URBAN TERRITORY AND PROPOSES A FINELY ARTICULATED SPATIAL STRATEGY OF BUILT AND UNBUILT ZONES THAT ENABLES GROWTH AND DEVELOPMENT.

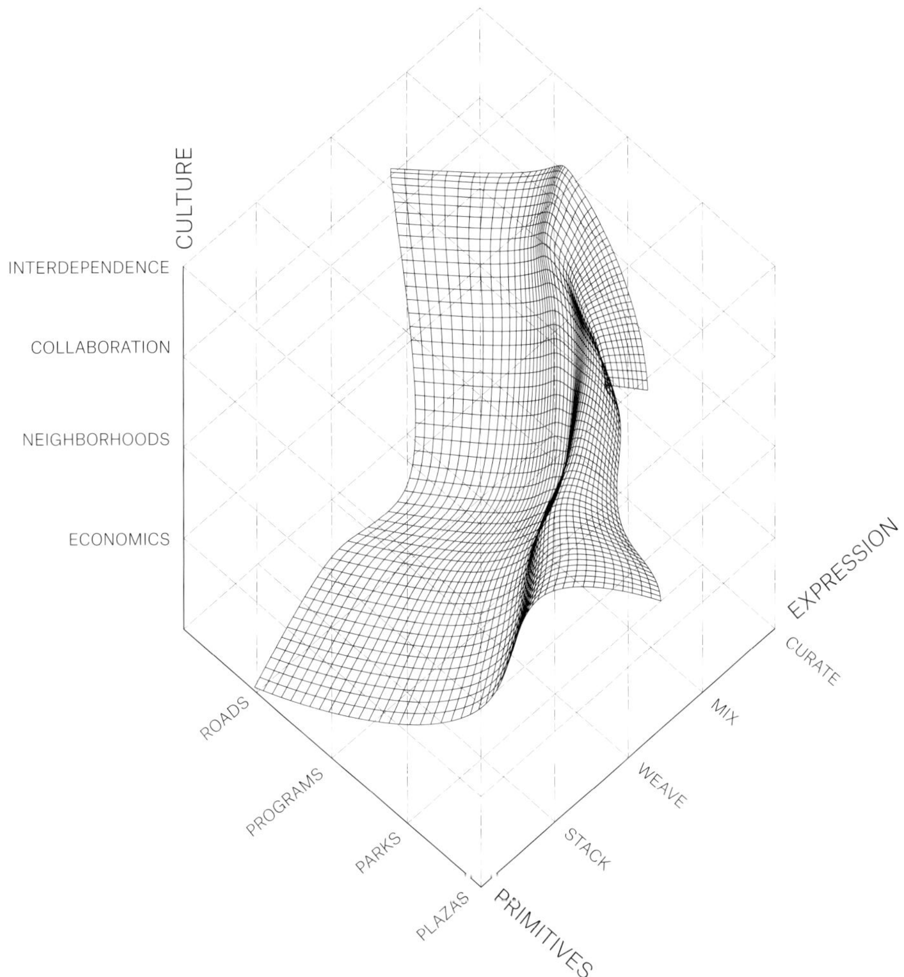

Plotting the Bogotá Centro Master Plan along the axes of cultural utility, primitive geometries, and formal expressions

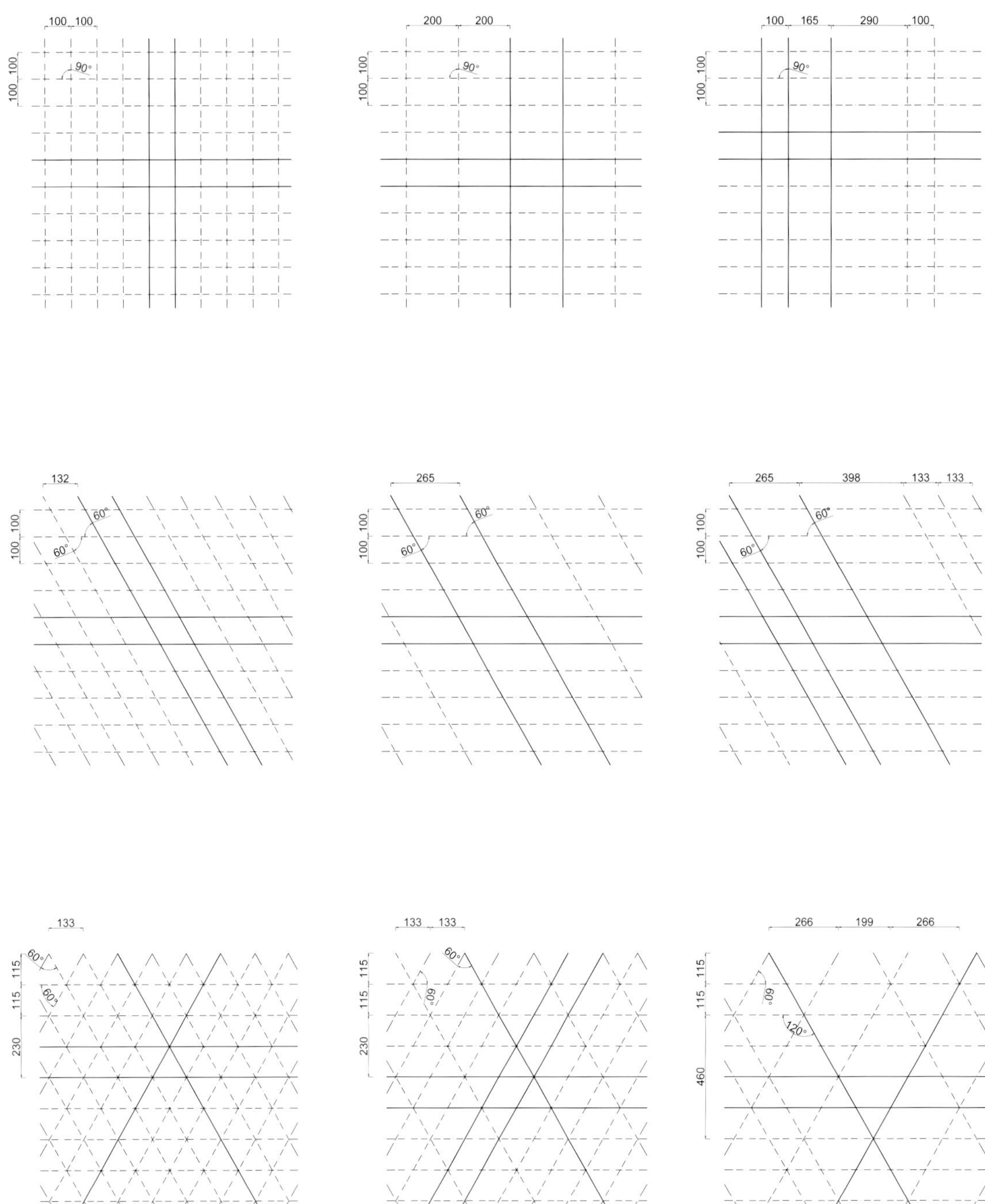

Plan studies producing new urban layouts based on existing grids in Bogotá

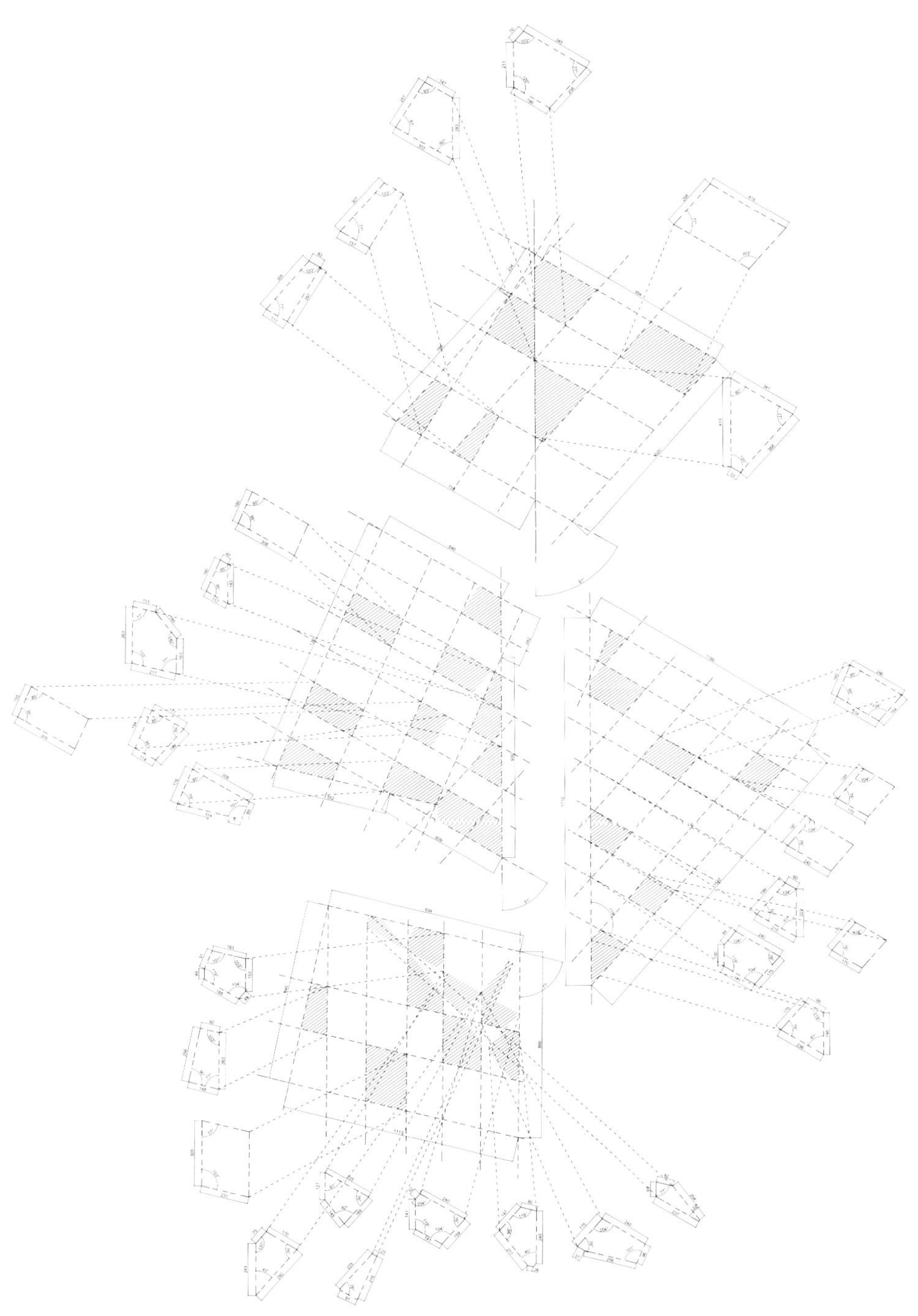

Diagram analyzing the overlay of street vectors from adjacent neighborhoods on the site

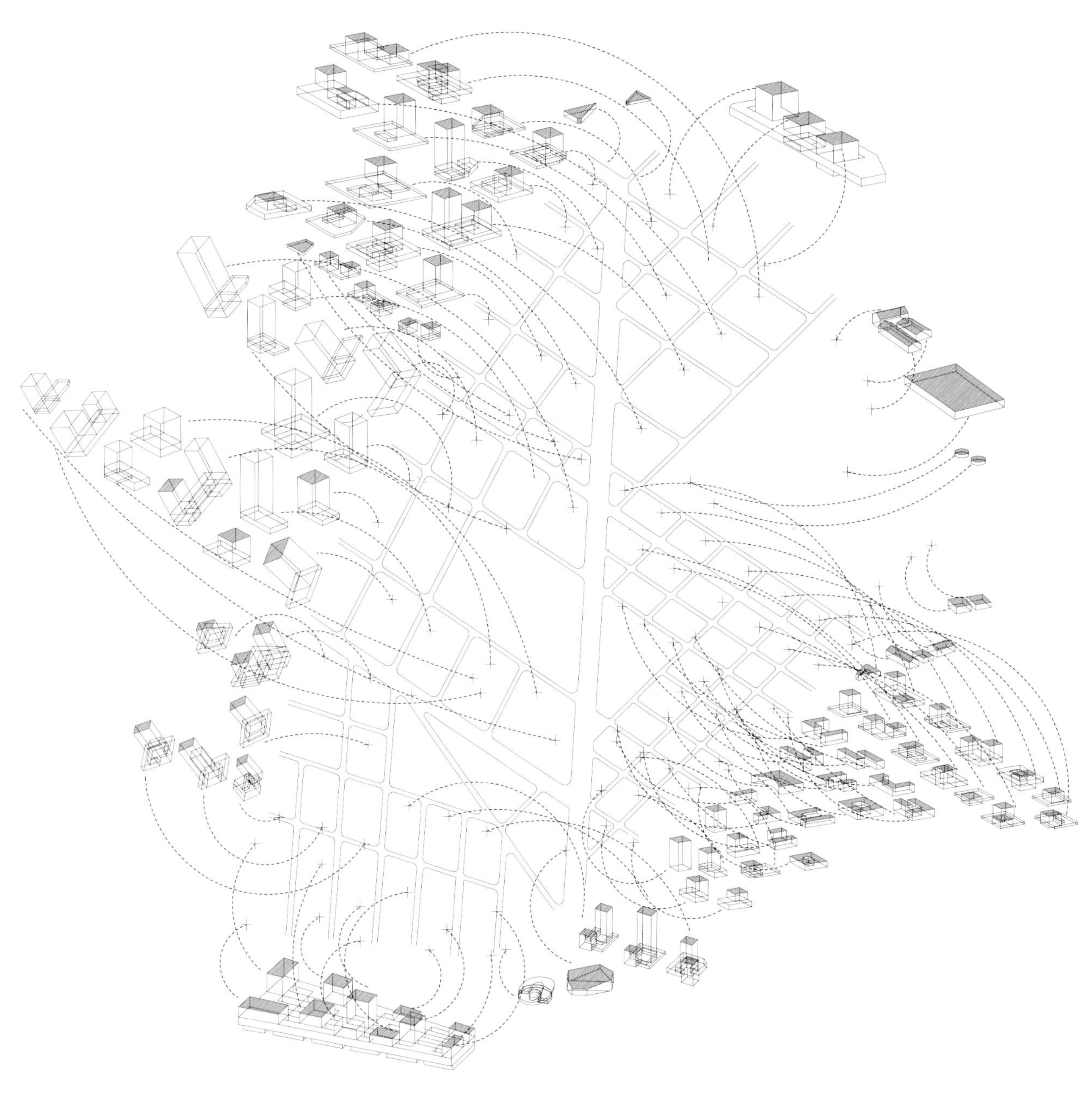

Developing a feedback loop to recycle known building types and produce different urban experiences

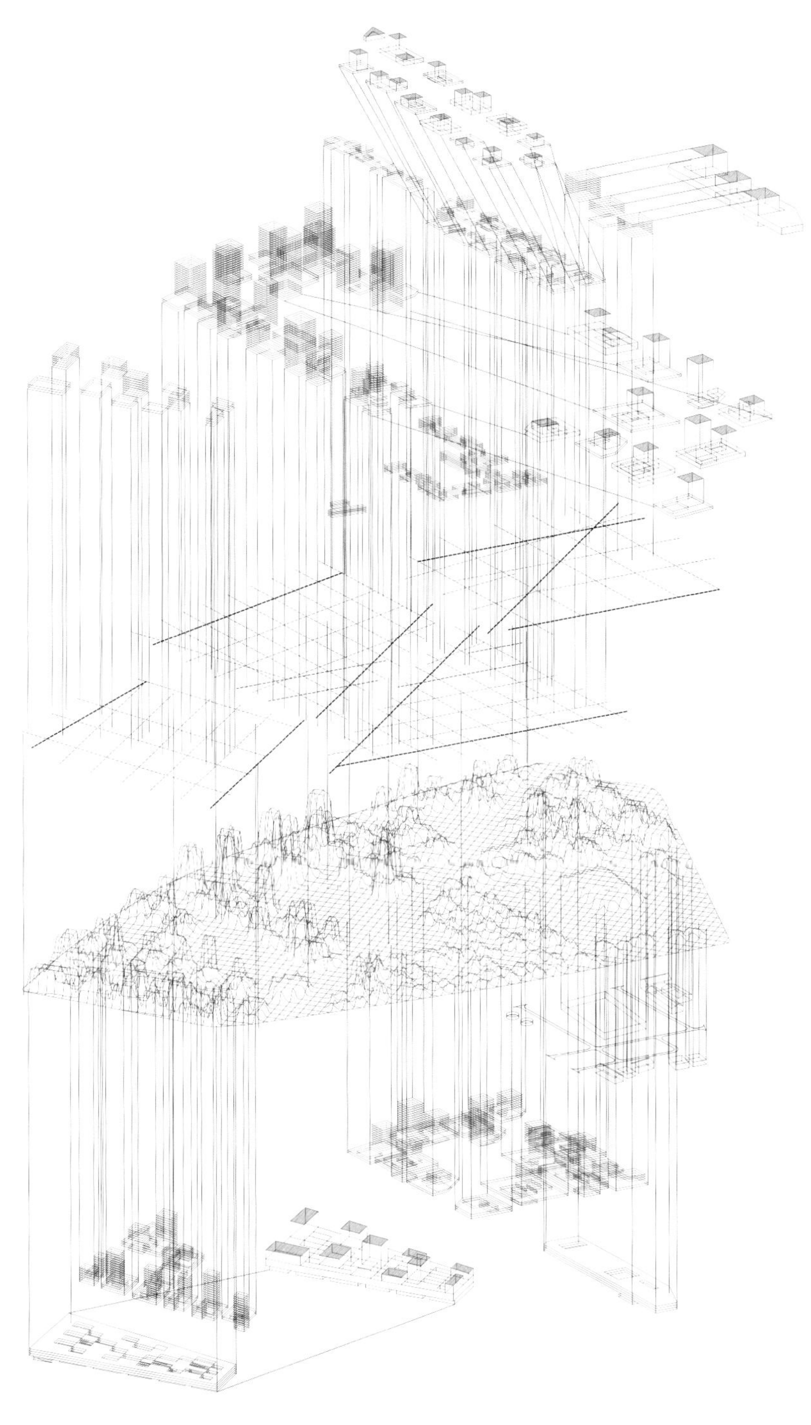

Exploded axonometric illustrating how the combination of building and open space creates a distinct identity for the Bogotá Centro

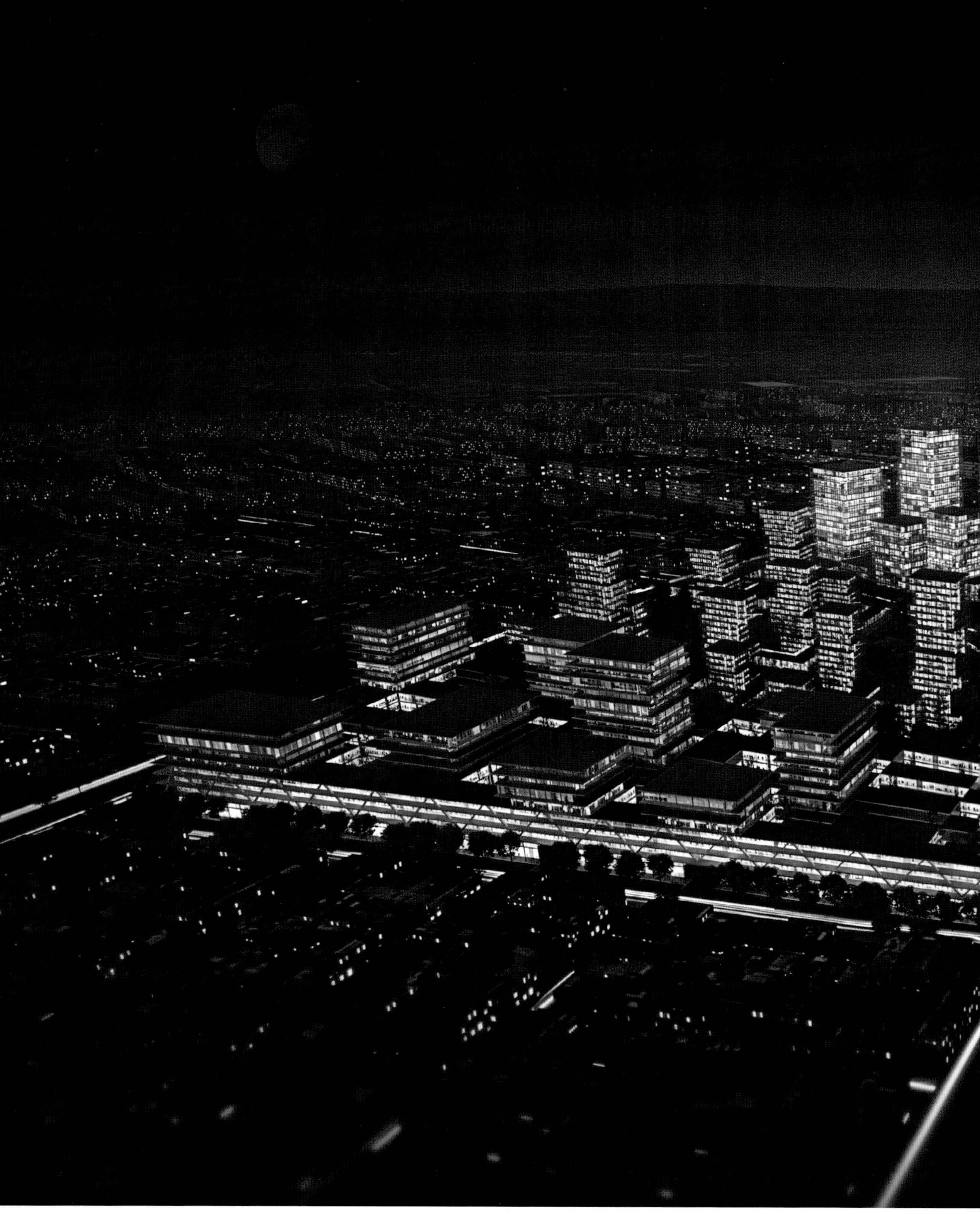

CITY CENTER TOWER

MANILA, PHILIPPINES

OUR DESIGN FOR CITY CENTER TOWER SOUGHT TO PUSH BACK AGAINST THE GEOMETRIC LIMITS OF THE STANDARD CORE AND SHELL OF A CORPORATE OFFICE BUILDING BY INTRODUCING A SERIES OF CONCENTRIC CIRCLES WITHIN THIS TRADITIONAL RECTANGULAR STRUCTURE. THE IMPACT VISUALLY MARRIES A MIXTURE OF STRUCTURED AND FREE-FORM SHAPES THAT ELICIT BOTH EFFICIENCY AND PLAYFULNESS. IT SATISFIES THE TENANT REQUIREMENTS, WHILE AT THE SAME TIME PRODUCING A FAÇADE POPULATED BY A SERIES OF BALCONIES AND BULGING METALLIC MULLIONS THAT HELP THE TYPICALLY CLOSED OFFICES ON THE INTERIOR LOOK OUT TO FIND A PARTICULAR PLACE AND TIME.

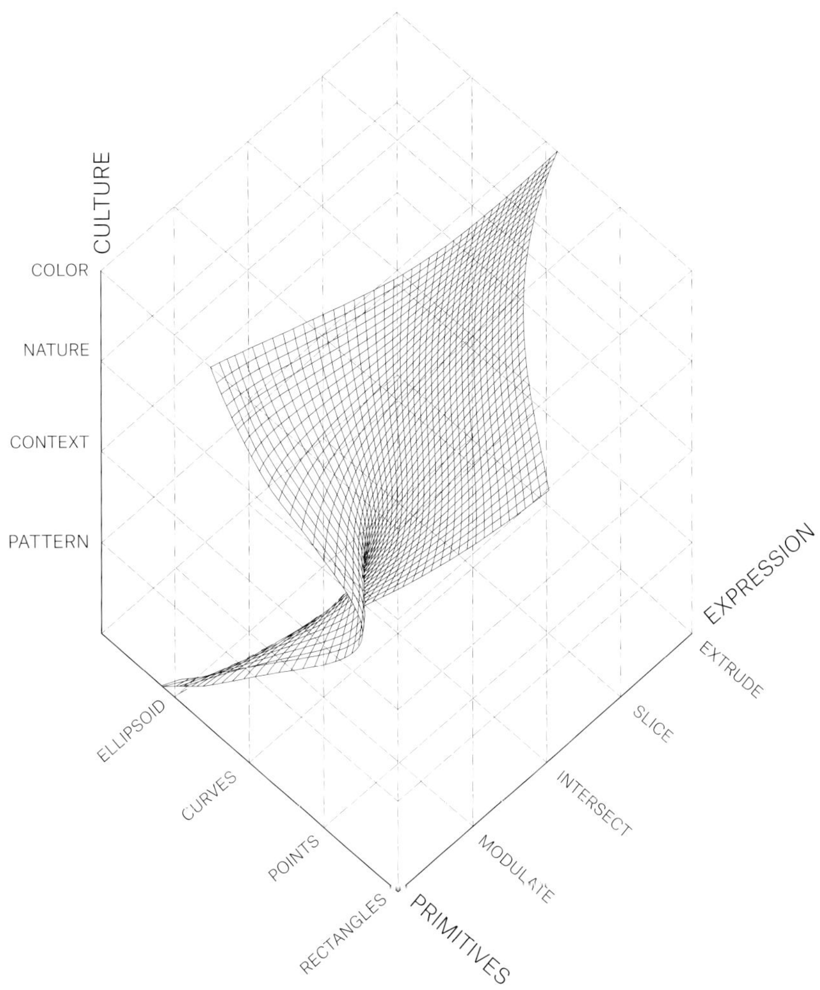

Plotting City Center Tower along the axes of cultural utility, primitive geometries, and formal expressions

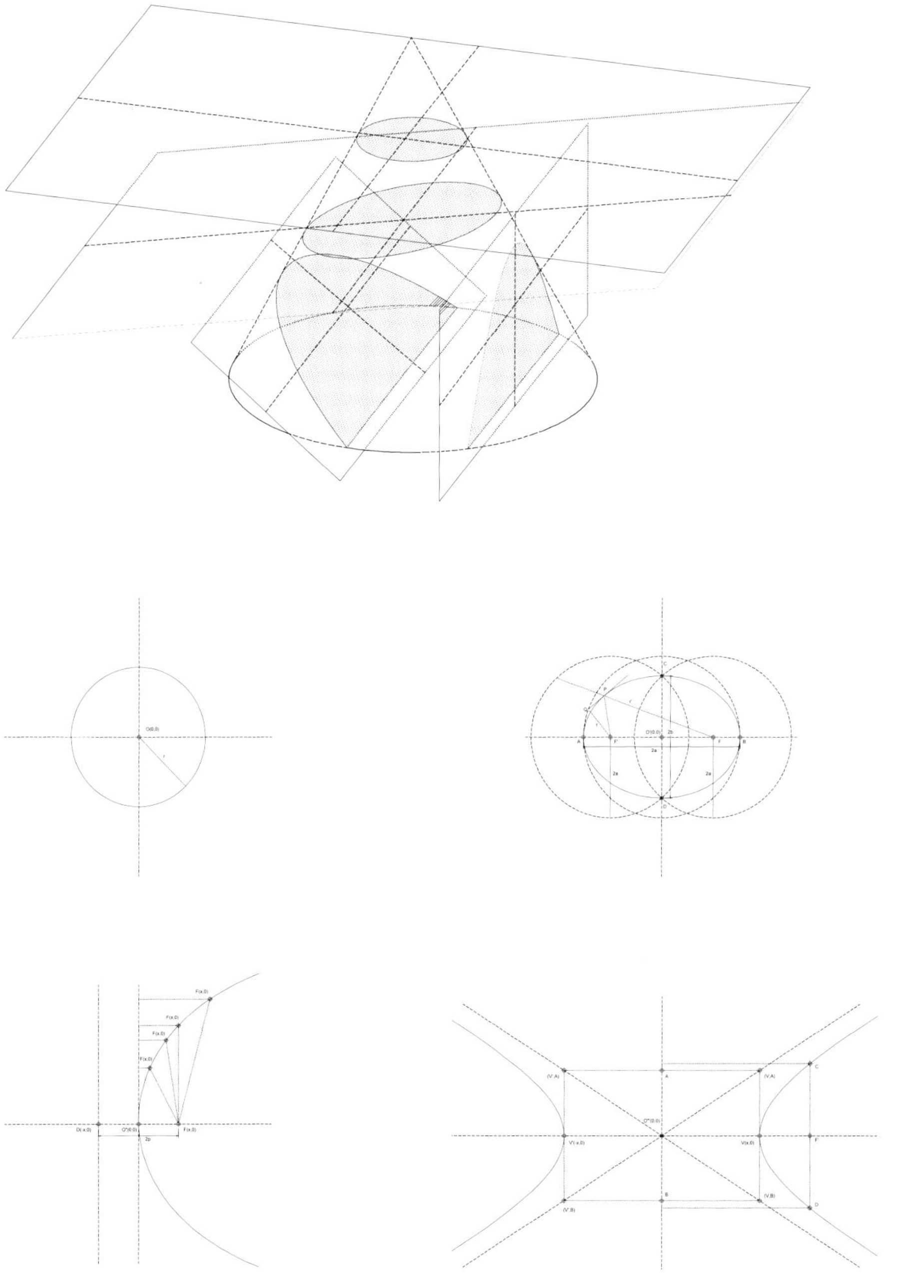

Studies into how a parabola intersects another shape and creates something unexpected

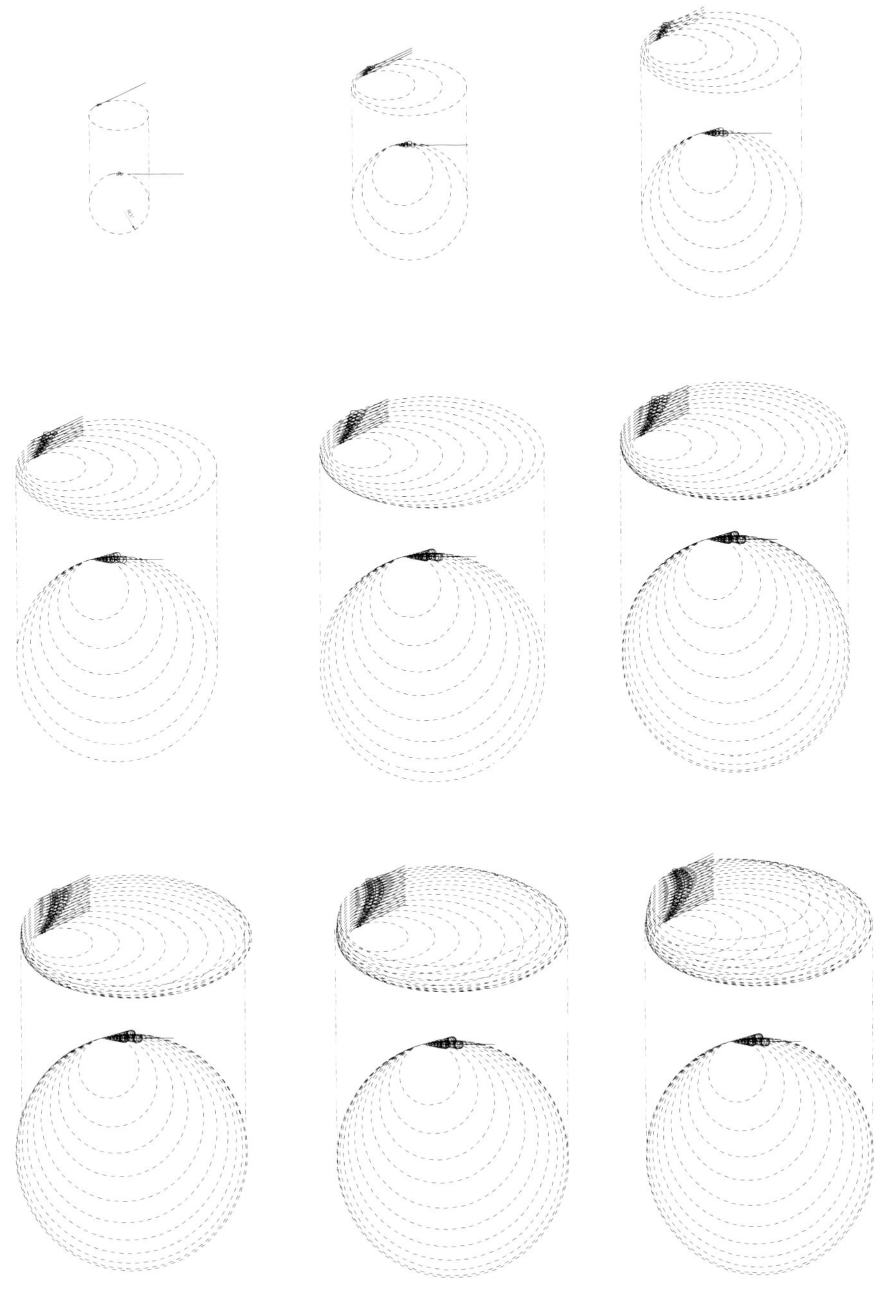

Illustration of a floor-by-floor intersection between a parabola and a rectangular shape

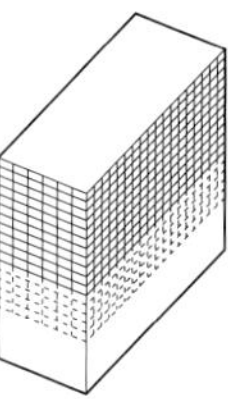

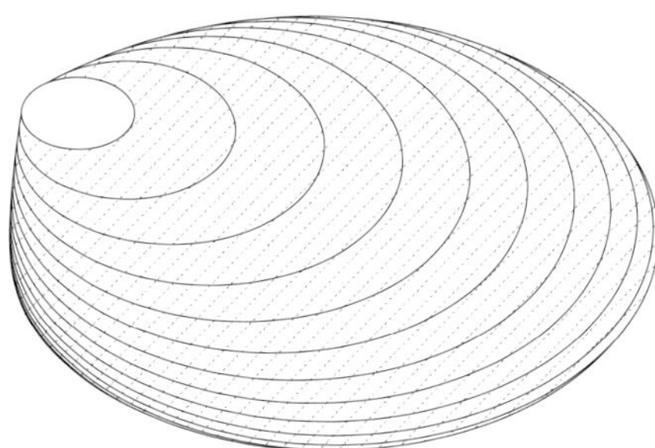

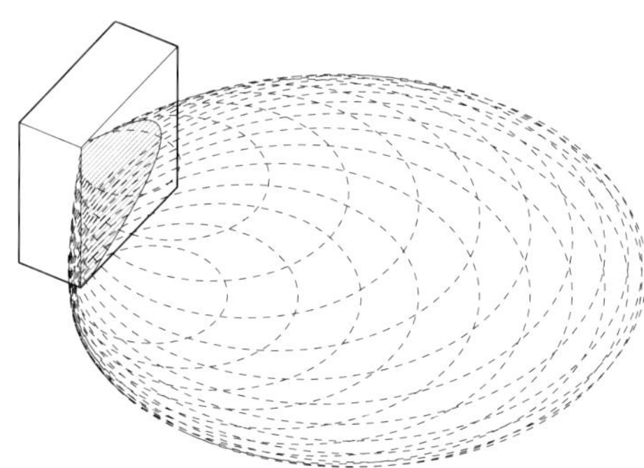

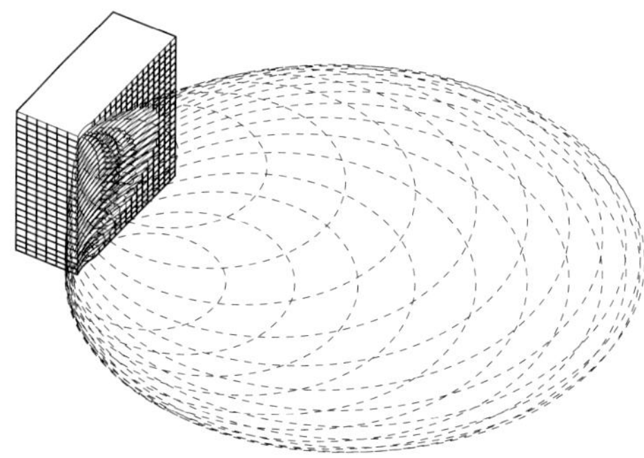

Diagram showing the change in the building skin when the parabola leaves its impression on the Tower

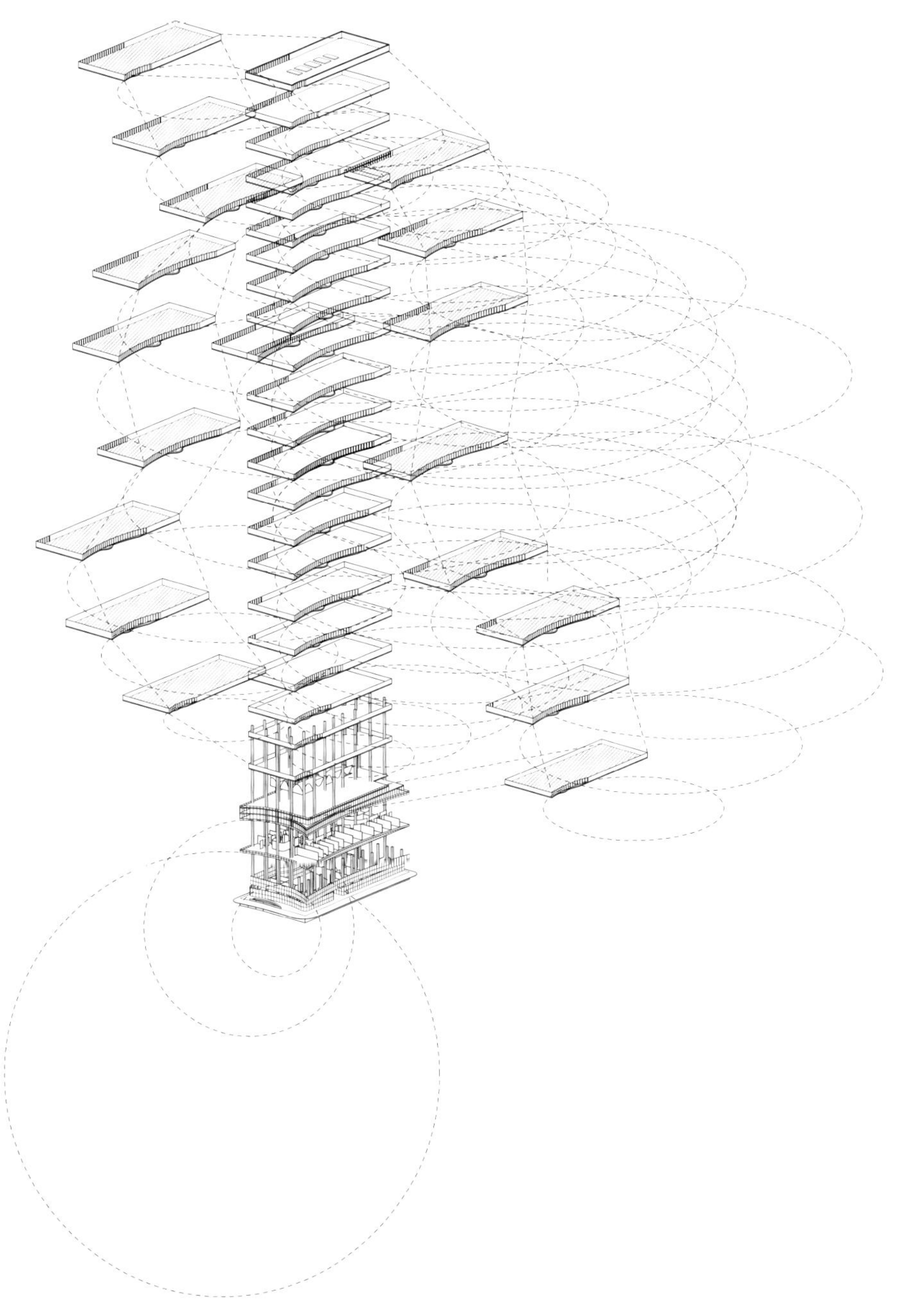

Exploded axonometric showing how the parabolic indentation creates a secondary network of public terraces on the extension of the City Center Tower

HUE HOTEL

BORACAY, PHILIPPINES

OUR AMBITION WAS TO RETHINK THE CONCEPT OF A BOUTIQUE HOTEL AND TROPICAL ARCHITECTURE FOR THE 21ST CENTURY. EMBRACING THE LUSH CLIMATE, BUT DRAWING ATTENTION INWARD, THE BULBOUS DESIGN COMPRISES A STACK OF INTERLOCKING RINGS PRODUCING A CONTINUAL, RHYTHMIC CYCLE OF ENTERTAINMENT AND RELAXATION THROUGH TERRACES, ROOF GARDENS, AND HOTEL AMENITIES. THE EXPERIENCE MOVES FROM COMMUNAL, RECREATIONAL SPACES IN THE CENTRAL ENCLOSURE TO A COLLECTION OF BESPOKE GUEST ROOMS ALONG THE UPPER REACHES OF THE BUILDING.

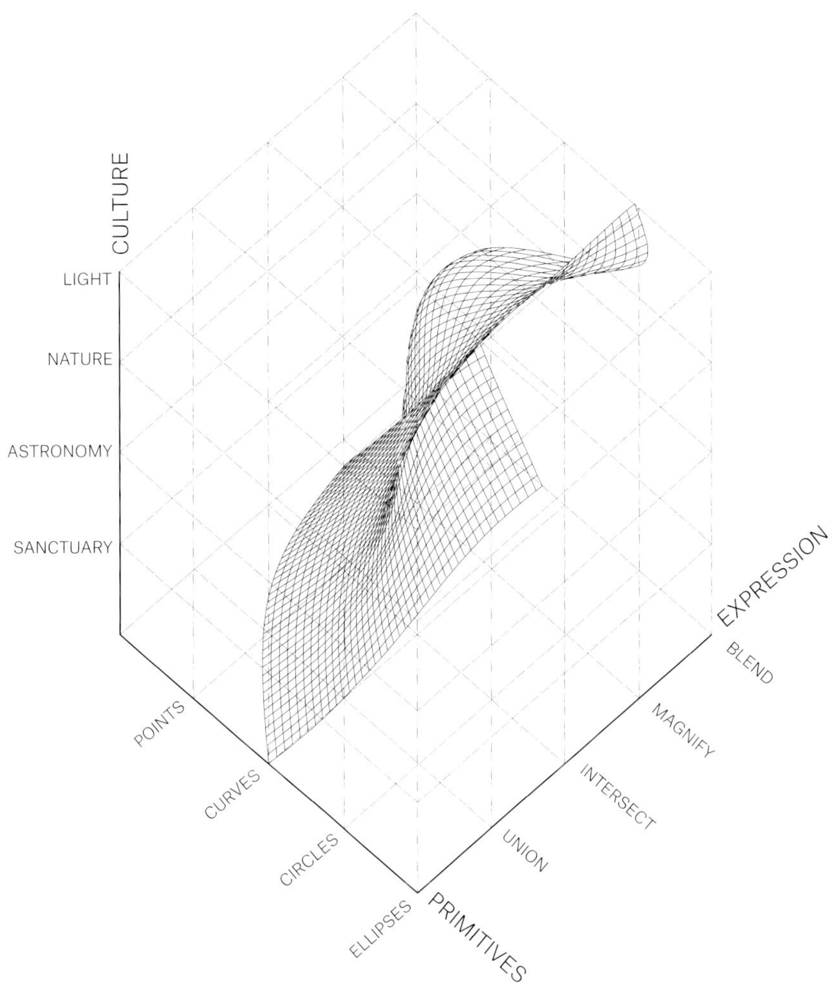

Plotting the Hue Hotel along the axes of cultural utility, primitive geometries, and formal expressions

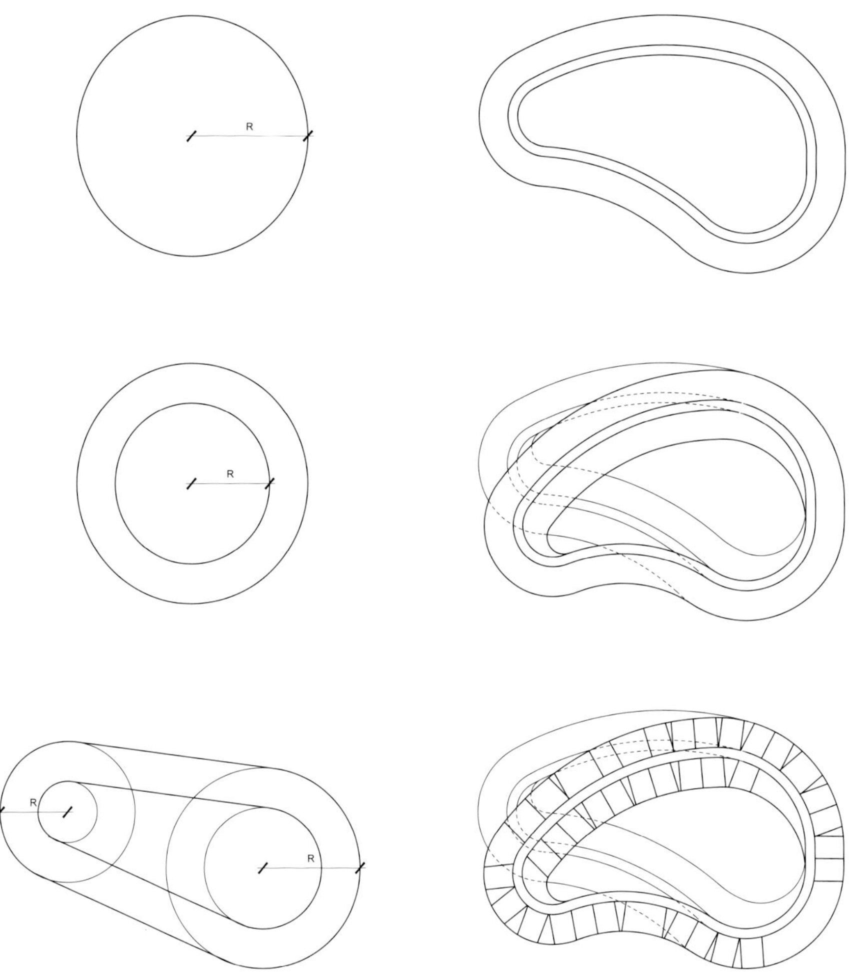

Studies of how two interconnected loops synthesize the private
and public worlds of the Hotel

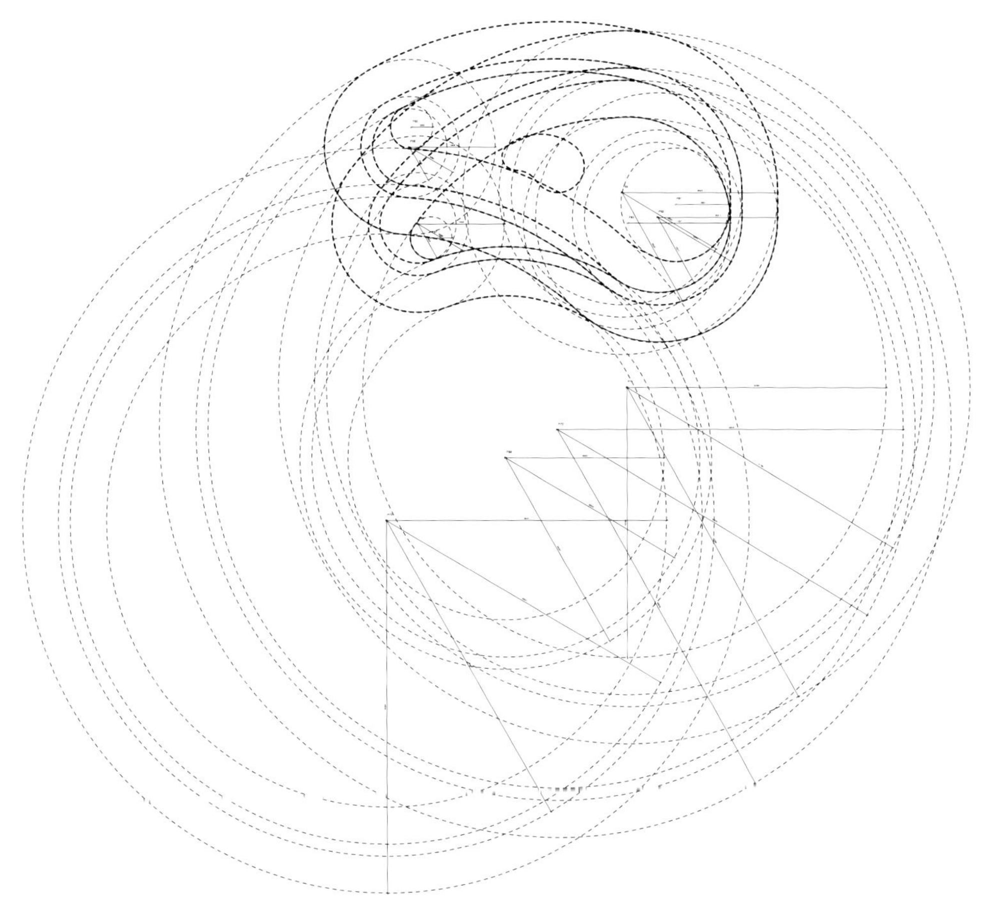

Diagrams illustrating the organizing logic of the multiple overlapping circles and loops in the Hotel

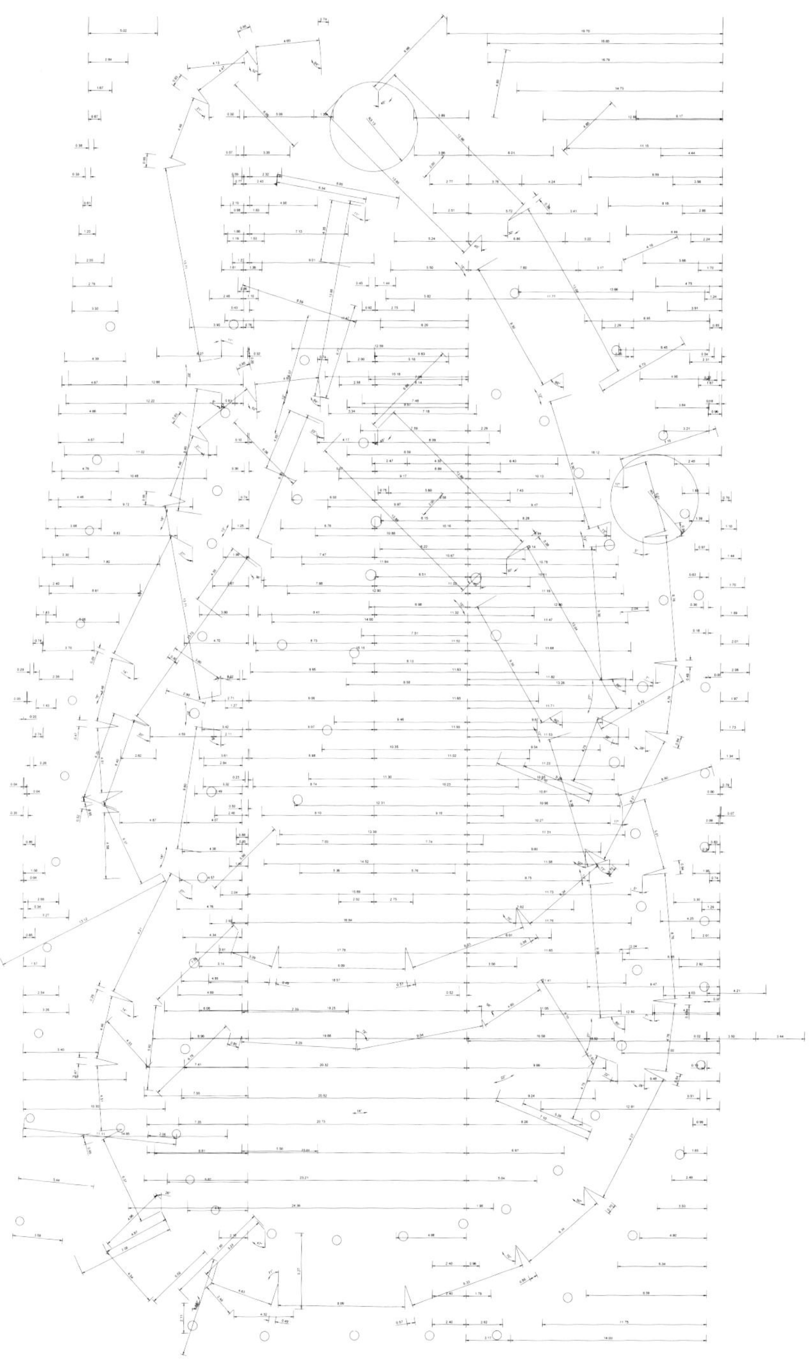

Exploring how the loops produce bulbous edges that define gardens, pavilions, and the Hotel pool

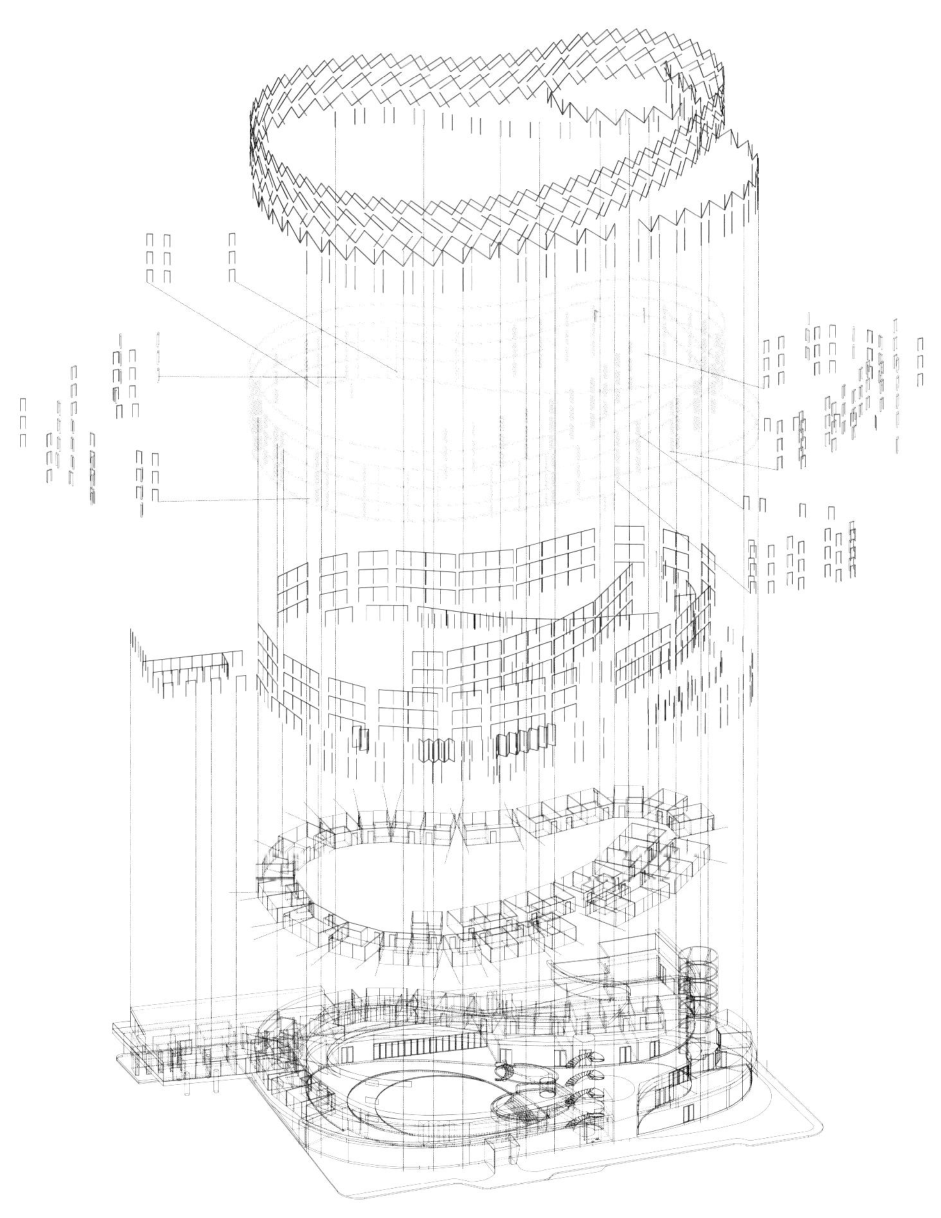

Exploded axonometric showing the different architectural systems in the Hue Hotel

MAKING THE SHOT WHILE FALLING: ON IVERSONIAN BEAUTY

CARLOS ARNAIZ

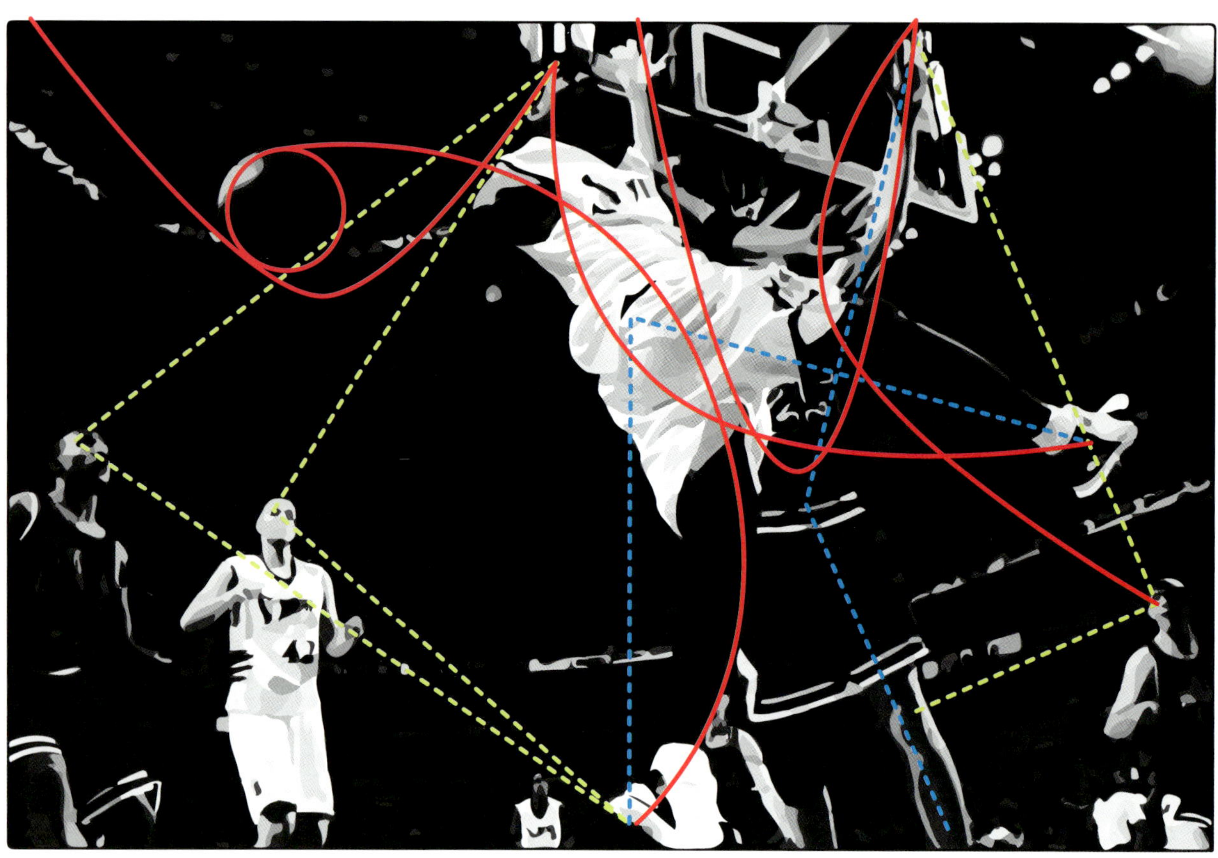

Diagram of Iversonian movement

Something beautiful fills the mind yet invites the search for something beyond itself, something larger or something of the same scale with which it needs to be brought into relation.
—Elaine Scarry

Beauty is political not despite the fact that it feels subjective but precisely because it is, in fact, subjective. Beauty enters us into a world of dispute, contention and conflict at the very moment when we feel to be removed from the social world... beauty exists at the tense intersection of the individual and society, with the individual neither fully subsumed nor fully free from social norms and cultural hierarchies . . . beauty is not something given but something that we do and something that we change.
—Dave Beech

The professional basketball player Allen Ezail Iverson played a different kind of game. He was shorter than most of his peers yet insisted on going deep into the court to score. His speed was legendary and his trajectory never straight. He would spin back and forth in a dizzying staccato of repetitive corkscrews, testing the field in front of him then leaving his opponents flat-footed. His most famous points were made while he was almost tumbling down to the ground.

Iverson's movements were almost like those of a frenetic 3-D printer. He tracked every possible play without predetermination then orchestrated a rapid blend of actions that left everyone—including, sometimes, himself—in shock. His game seemed based on the recognition of emergent patterns instead of on the execution of a preconceived plan. Iverson's form felt nearly digital. His breakthrough was in being able to make athletic opportunities through a variable nonlinear probabilistic process.

Iverson on the court looked as if he was actively learning to play. He appeared to be sampling the environment for new forms. His game was arresting because there was something about it that we recognized yet didn't know or anticipate. His basketball was a kind of exercise in restless prototyping. This probably explains his proximity to failure. His successful moves exemplified a promise, at the level of the imagination, that the game might be played otherwise.

Watching Iverson play is an altogether contemporary experience of the beautiful. His game is not concerned with idealized form. His basketball is beautiful because, rather than being a thing in itself, it suggests that the sport is a game about the immediate world around us. Iverson's plays demand an extension of one's experience. They are models to think of athletic form as a discursive practice that connects us with the basketball court in unpredictable ways.

Our contemporary experience of architecture is not dissimilar to Iversonian basketball. Buildings cannot be isolated from their surroundings and as such any concept of architectural beauty cannot be autonomous from the world. We cannot assume unmediated knowledge of our surroundings and our sense of enduring exile is a given in our post-humanist age of continual crises. Our buildings are similarly part of their context but not altogether integrated: building systems are widely parcelized, the construction industry is Balkanized, and the execution of any project involves multiple constituents seeking consensus through design.

The whale of social media and electronic exchange has swallowed architecture. Buildings today are no longer objects of contemplation or even unmitigated distraction. We see them proliferate as images on screens dissolving their solid mass of material realism. Our image-driven economy treats buildings as proxies for future investment scenarios. Architecture in the age of unremitting online declaratives and multi-player video games has become an open interface for the emergence of infinite publics.

Architectural beauty today is less and less actualized in any particular shape. Visit any famous building and witness how the flow of digital information mediates architectural form: countless people frantically snapping pictures to send instead of stricken still, as Odysseus once was, when confronted with the beautiful. Our contemporary relationship with architecture is entirely rhizomatic. We seek out connections and are drawn to objects because of their ability to relate to other objects.

Umberto Eco's comparative treatise on the history of beauty established its inexorable mutability. Beauty, we learned, is not absolute. Its diverse history is directly dependent on our changing models of the universe. Any reflection on contemporary beauty is, therefore, a consideration of the language we have to discourse our world. If this is so, contemporary architectural beauty might then be a node in a network connecting our concepts of aesthetic judgment to ideas about our environment, our political precariousness, our economic volatility, and ultimately ourselves.

The Western philosophical tradition of beauty when applied to architecture, however, has had the effect of separating the beautiful building from its surroundings. Plato's cave established beauty as an approximation of an idealized environment. Buildings are, as a consequence, turned into shadows of a perfection we partially glimpse through an encounter with the beautiful. Aristotle's paradigm of organic unity set up beauty as complete, which in turn makes it impossible to define architectural beauty in terms of a building's engagement with any fluctuating spatiotemporal phenomenon such as light. Immanuel Kant's expression of the beautiful as "disinterested delight" further separated buildings from the actuality of our daily engagement with architecture. Beauty's irresistibility thus confirmed architecture's autonomy.

The Iversonian model of basketball calls for an understanding of beauty based on how individuals relate to a changing field of forces in front of them. Playing basketball like Iverson becomes an exercise in the generation of new positions, rather than a rerun of known forms. The beautiful in architecture must similarly be conceived of as a creative act of ideation. The appearance of things in architecture is inseparable from their working in the world and as such any discussion of beauty in architecture is an engagement with a conceptual framework about buildings and their physical and cultural milieu.

The trouble is that architectural beauty does not tell us what it is about. Beauty does not involve a didactic transmission of ideas. We know it when we see it. To encounter beauty is to become instantly acquainted with the mental event of conviction, as Elaine Scarry wondrously documented in her readings of the beautiful from Homer through Rilke. The experience of the beautiful is an experience of momentary buoyancy that insinuates itself as a discernibly exuberant event.

We see Iverson make the shot and feel something that leads to a declaration. Beauty begets pleasure that in turn creates a desire for communication. The beautiful in architecture becomes an invitation to describe that which lies beyond us. Like Einstein's theory of how stars are made, beauty demands the creation of its own space. The crystallization of beauty exemplifies a triumph in our ability to connect with our built environment and to take delight in our imaginary exploration of this outside.

Hans-Georg Gadamer's essay on the relevance of the beautiful imparts a model for thinking of beauty as a discursive event of transgression. The beautiful is an activity centered on the possibility of exceeding the logic of current systems of thought. Architectural beauty is a proxy to play with our limits as individuals. Play, for Gadamer, is how we create community through communication. The beautiful challenges us "to constructnew compositions directly from the elements of the objective visible world and to participate in the profound tensions that they set up . . . it challenges each of us to listen to the language in which the world speaks and to make it our own."

Contemporary architectural beauty offers up the possibility to think of connectivity as an optimistic gesture. We not only discern something clearly but we are provoked to deliberate. We want to make connections back and forth with other places both real and imagined. The beautiful creates the desire to relate buildings to their contexts and histories—it is a rouse to experience architecture as part of a community of people.

Robin Evans once described his encounter with the Barcelona Pavilion as an experience that focused our attention on how see. This is an example of beauty producing a concept. Encountering the beautiful in contemporary architecture can be like meeting Gilles Deleuze's friend of wisdom, whose "presence is intrinsic to thought, a condition of possibility of thought itself—in short, a living category, a constitutive element of thought."

The beautiful in architecture transforms our built environment into a repository of possible ideas about how things work and why they can be different. Experiencing beauty makes us momentarily like Iverson on the basketball court. It is an alchemical process of conceptualization that sets up a tension between facts and experience. We can talk about new perfections in the work of Álvaro Siza and Kazuyo Sejima or different truths in projects by Jacques Herzog and Pierre de Meuron or partial multiplicities in buildings by Enric Miralles. These architects produce singularities that acknowledge their contingent situation, reordering reality in ways that are both enduring and touching.

Beauty is an activity of creating concepts in architecture. Concepts do not wait. To actualize a new world through design is to be engaged in the production of imagined communities. We live in an age that exalts the frenetic as it produces a wondrous improbability that is distinct from the silence and coherence of the sublime. Our expectations are constantly bombarded by what can happen as a result of the fact that our world has been exposed as incomplete. Our designs must be made in response to this static-filled reality. We must try, like Iverson, to imagine how we can move through space in improbable ways and make the shot even while we are falling down. If the beautiful in contemporary architecture has an optimistic structure, its optimism lies in the awareness that empathy results from the desire to transform our improbable physical environment into a cultural space of exchange.

WORK SPACE

LUKE BULMAN

Product: X-LED LINE
Product: tectum m
Position: every or every second crossing point of vertical and horizontal pipes
Aiming: upwards
INNOVATIVE LIGHTING SOLUTIONS

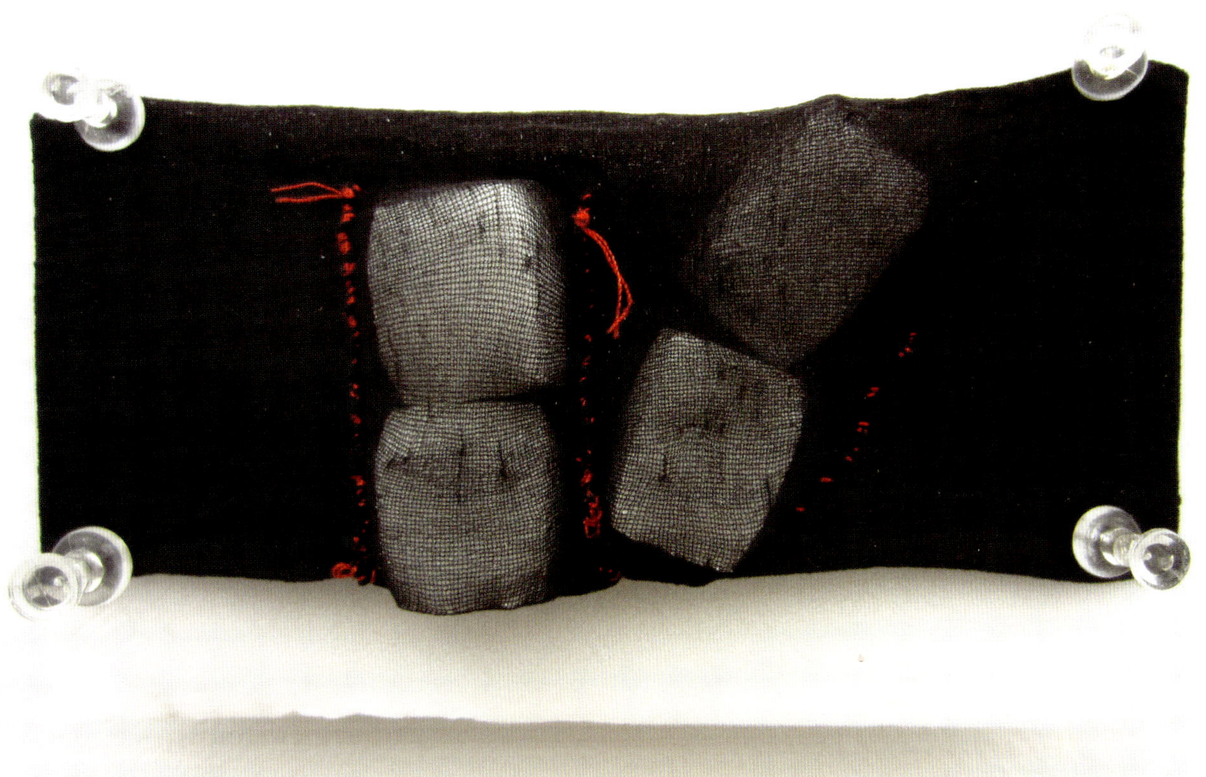

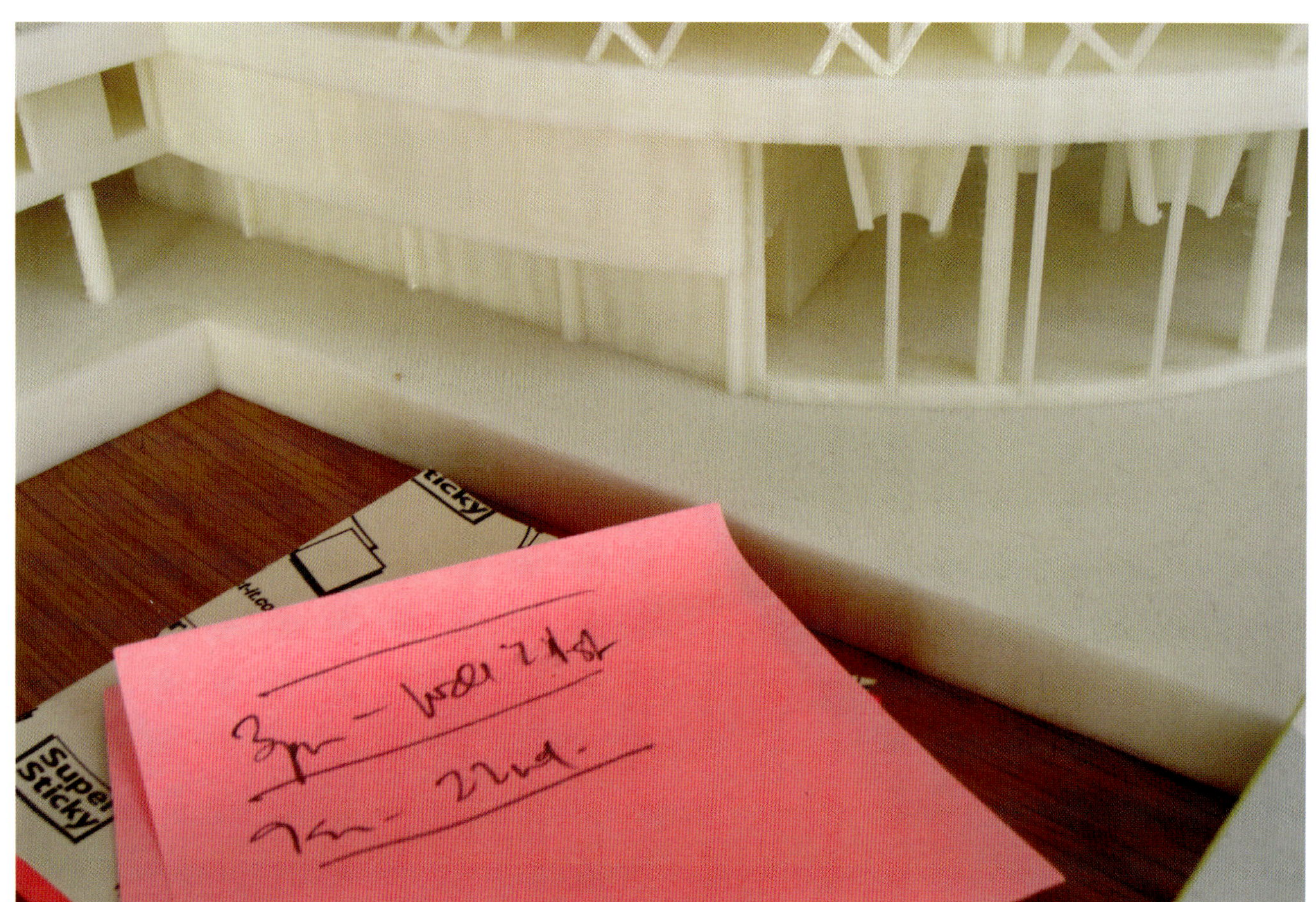
Super
Sticky

Interaction of Color
50th Anniversary Edition
010

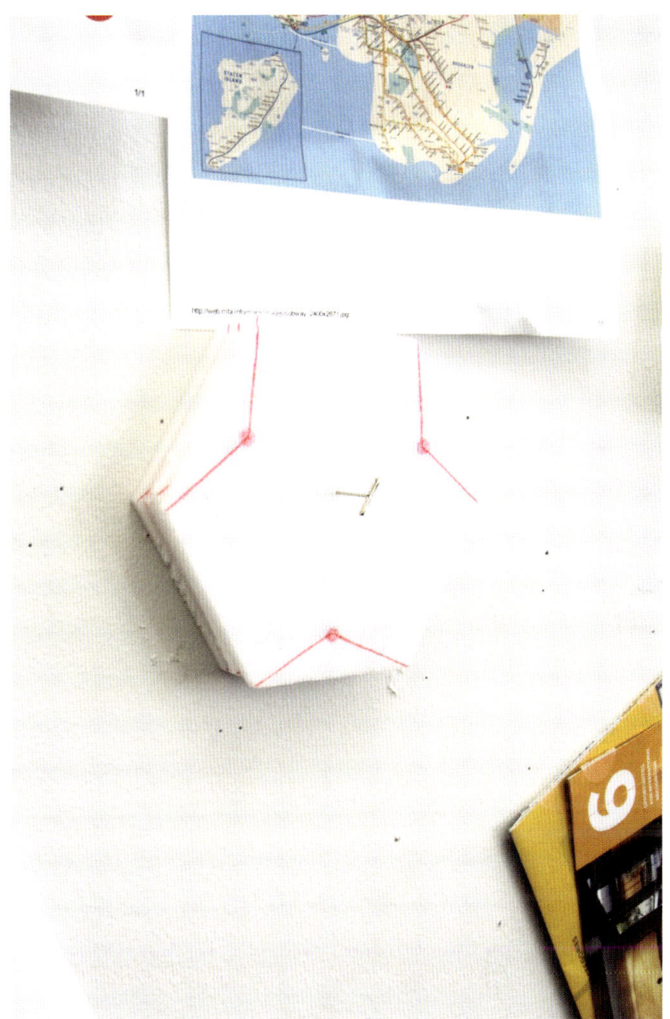

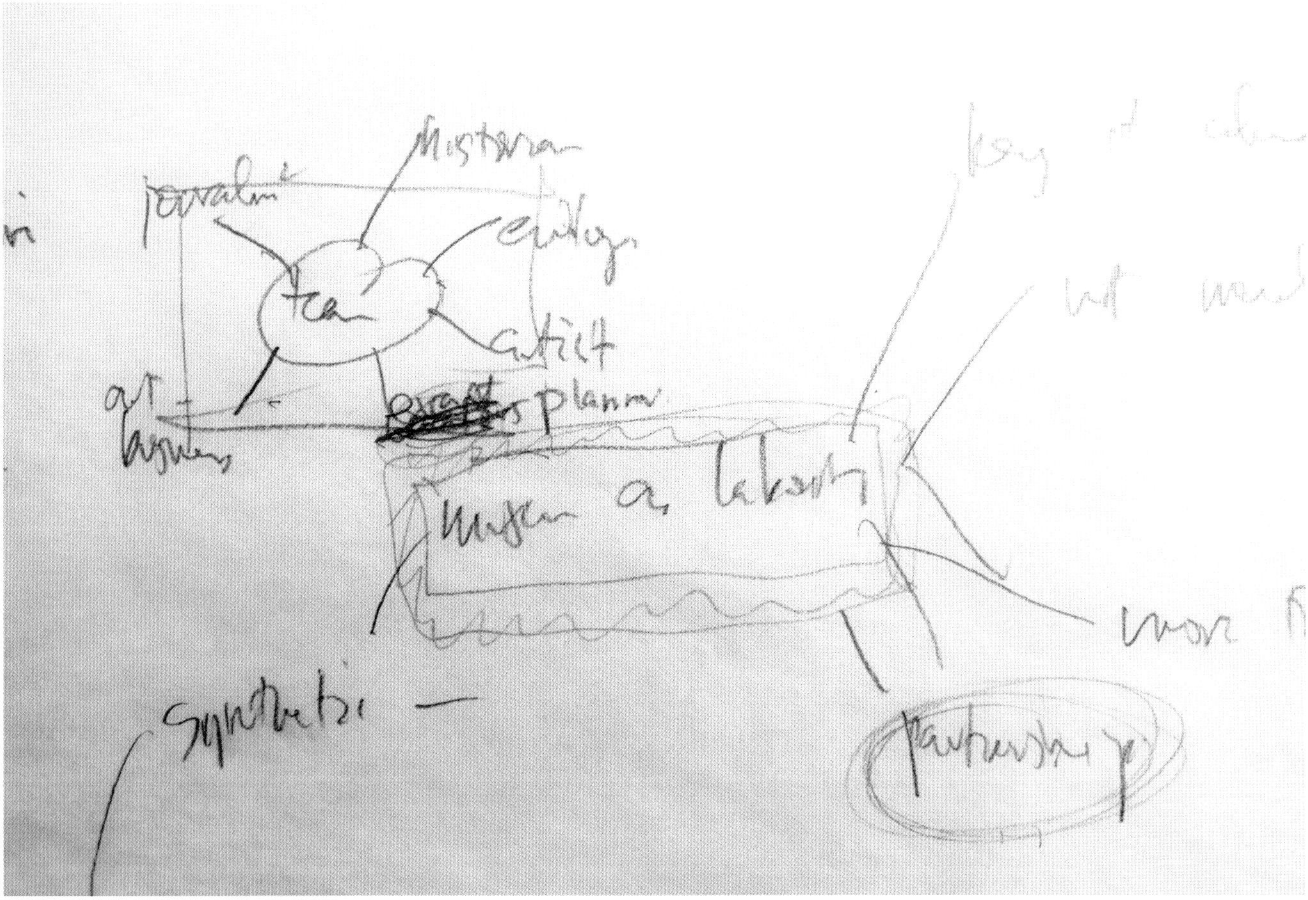

historian

journalist

ecologist

team

artist

art designers

planner

museum as laboratory

more

synthesize

partnership

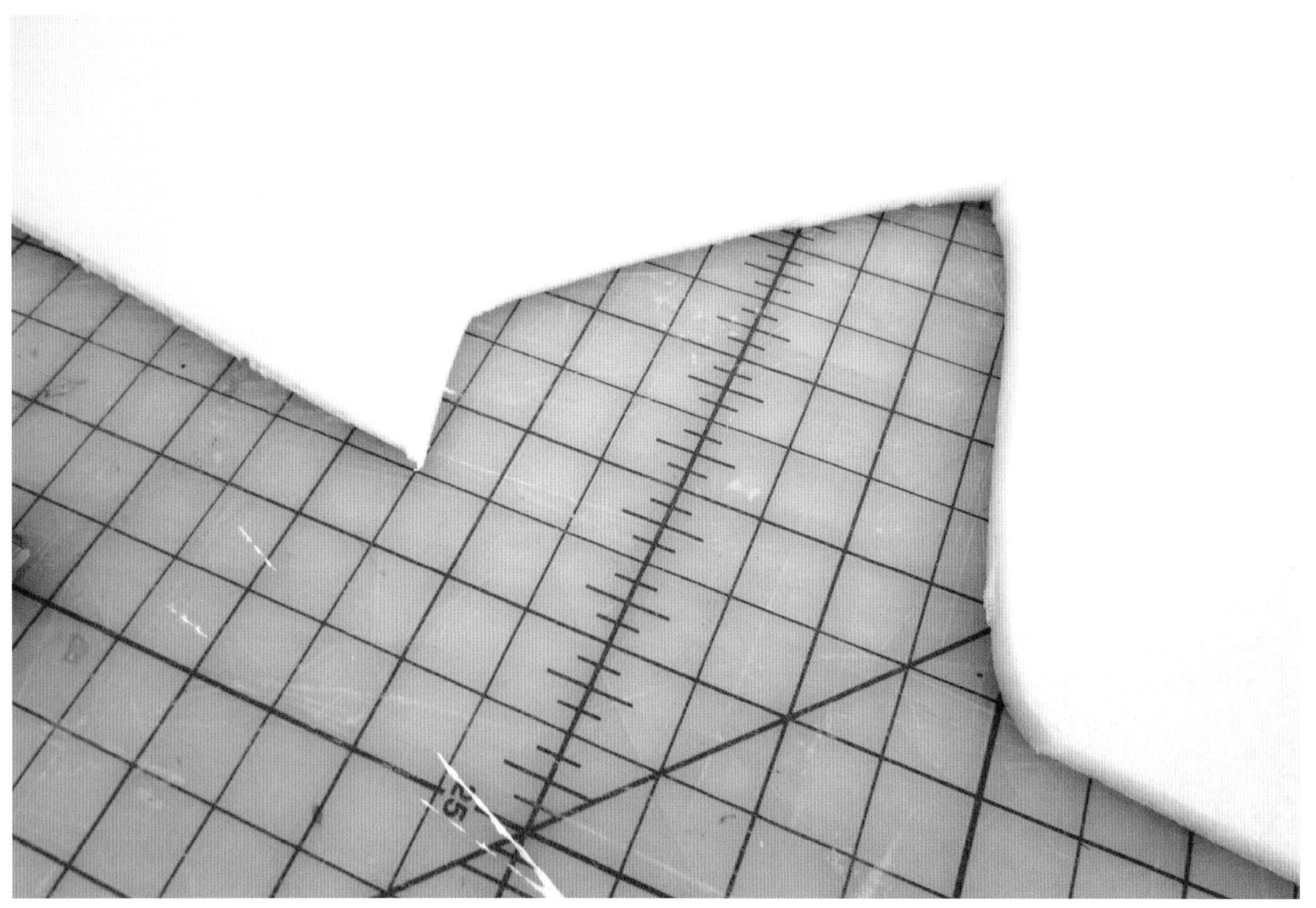
25

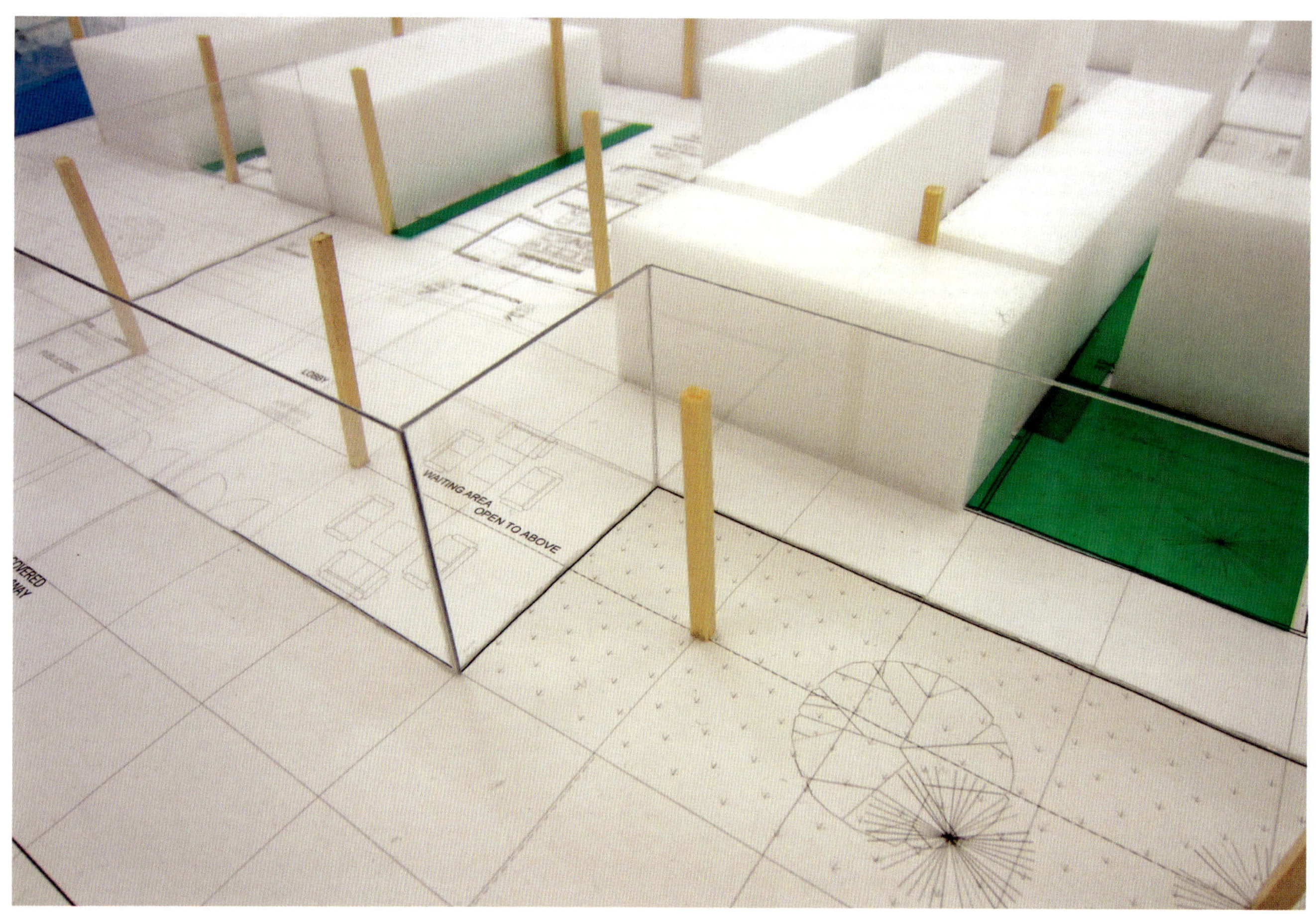
LOBBY
WAITING AREA
OPEN TO ABOVE

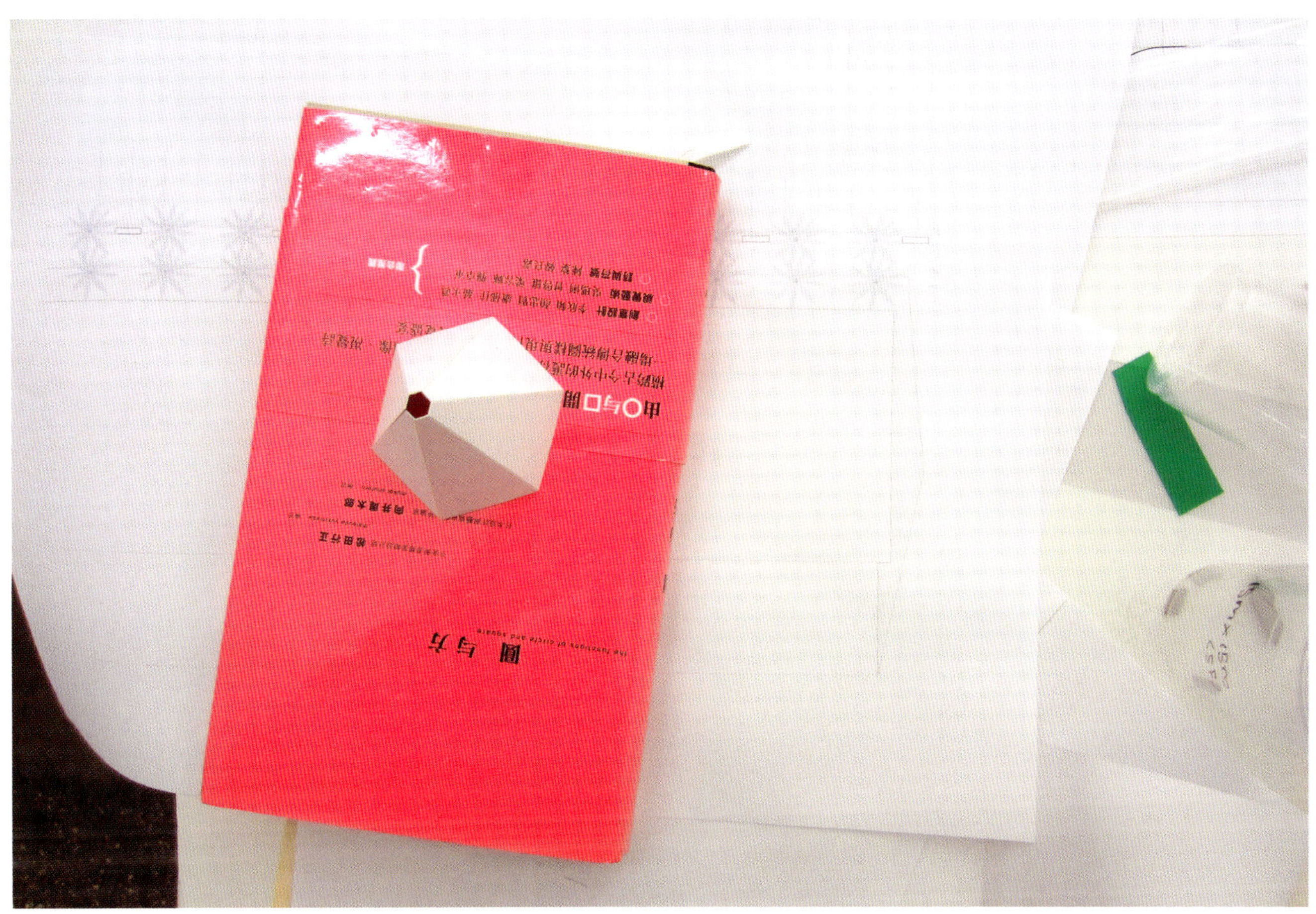

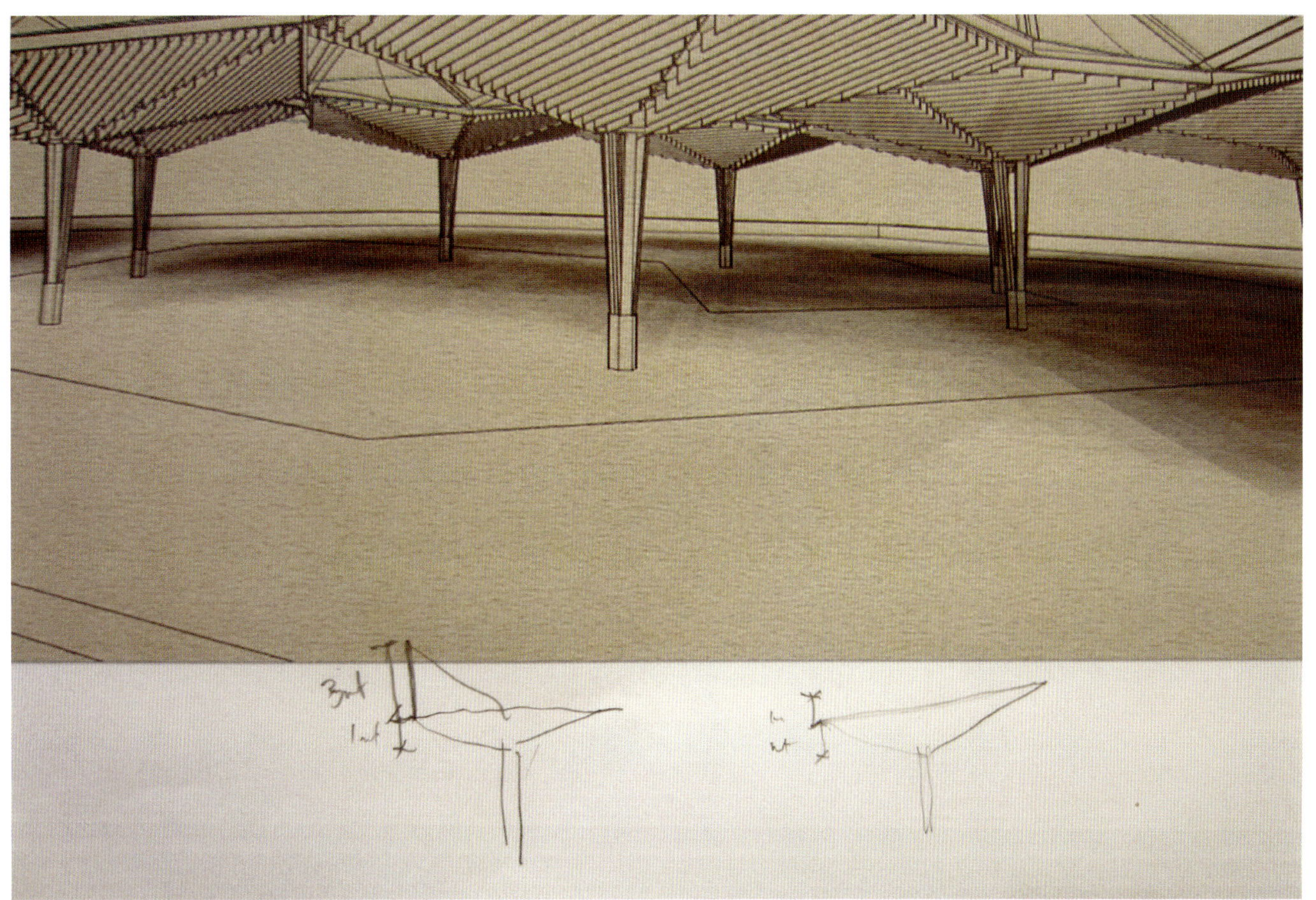

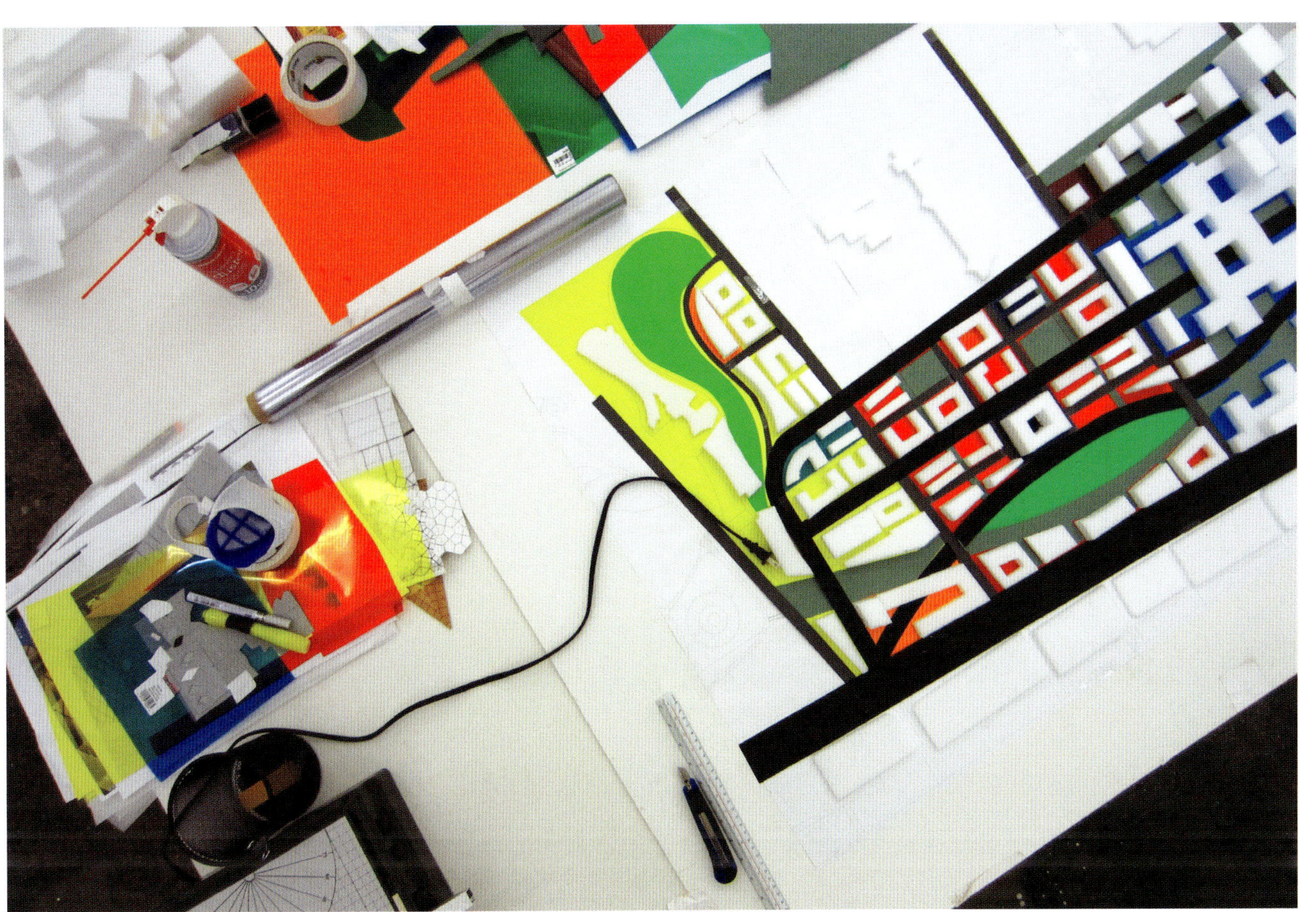

CONVERSATIONS

ON URBANISM

ON GEOMETRY

ON COMMUNICATION

ARNAIZ So this is one project I thought you'd find interesting. It's in Bogotá. It's currently an existing brewery for the largest beer company in Colombia. It measures 72 hectares and is the largest open piece of land in Bogotá. So we basically started off by extending the grid, creating a series of patchwork neighborhoods that come from the existing grain of the streets, and then slipping in these series of little dots. So that's what you end up getting, these little islands of development with this series of green pearls. It gets tighter and lower toward the back. It gets a little higher usually toward the green zones. The typology changes along the main avenue. The retail gets mixed in at different scales, larger along the edges, dense and linear through the middle, creating a variegated network of commercial points and lines.

ROWE Funny that in Medellín, for example, what impressed me were these great big towers on lots where there'd be green around it. And where it wasn't green, like, tower and a park, it was like, tower and its park.

ARNAIZ A little park. Yeah. But they were all gated, right?

ROWE Oh yeah, and they should be.

ARNAIZ What's interesting, actually, is that even these lower-middle-class housing developments are all gated.

ROWE Hashim and I and a few other people at the GSD [Harvard Graduate School of Design] got into a huge argument the other day in the studio elements review vis-à-vis housing in Manhattan—the one that ends on Jefferson Park, it's a long strip of public housing that was done just slightly north of Central Park, '50s housing in a green setting. And the proposal was, we're going to fill up the green with public stuff. Hashim and I hit the roof. We said, "Hey, whoa, wait a minute. You don't understand. That's not public. That belongs to the housing." They said, "Well, yeah, it's fenced." We said, "Oh gee, I wonder why." It's like a complete misunderstanding of this tower-and-the-park thing. The park isn't public; it belongs to the bloody buildings. And of course it's fenced, it could be fenced better and so forth, that's not a problem socially. It's when you try to make that public that you've really got an issue, because what you're doing is you're depriving a group of people, in this case highly subsidized tenants, of the only piece of green space they can ever lay their mitts on. Things like Stuyvesant City were great. They put a wall around the whole damn thing. Stay out.

ARNAIZ There's an interesting question then: the two districts in Bogotá that are most desirable, where the housing prices are the highest, most resilient, are the ones where you have less green, and house towers tightly packed together. They're not large clusters. They produce these communities where you can park in your building's garage, walk out of your building, three blocks to a park or three blocks to a commercial zone.

ROWE That's just a stratification question. We have that in New York too. I live in SoHo and no damn park anywhere near me.

ARNAIZ But I'm curious. Could that model work for the middle class in developing cities?

ROWE In this day and age, probably not. They wouldn't go for it.

ARNAIZ Is it them who wouldn't go for it? Or is it really the development machine?

ROWE Both. One sells. The other one buys. They buy like, not this bandwidth but that. So the other thing that's making that work is, it's very exclusive. There are only two of these in the whole city. So it's a certain kind of person who gets there and says, "Oh, this is great." São Paulo is like that.

ARNAIZ Yes, exactly, similar to São Paulo. Little pockets, and the market is segmented, broken.

ROWE Segmented. All markets are segmented.

ARNAIZ Not for the middle class, because there you have much larger monopolies where you have one company that takes on 30 hectares and develops it and then puts up the fence.

ROWE But most markets, if they see themselves as being inherently tied together, will always converge toward a singularity. For example, we did a big empirical study on the diversity of housing in Shanghai. It had most variety in 1978, and you think, "What? That's weird." Not now, because in fact it converged around two types, because that's where the market is, as far as they're concerned, "they" being the developers. That can be a problem. That's where government agencies and other people need to step in and say, "Well, not necessarily."

The issue of private space in the city is a bit like the Russian doll. It's gated and it's separated. These guys are also separated because they can also have private space. So it's that within that, that within that. There needs to be some sort of story about the degree to which there's self-similarity or not between those various scales.

ARNAIZ That's something that we struggle with at CAZA.

ROWE In the Bogotá project, you've got pieces that are fabrics. Those fabrics will have intrinsic qualities and they might be quite a bit different, because you've got different building typologies. They will also have formations within the fabric that make it more lumpy. So you'll have individual lumpy fabric and then fabric to other fabrics in field situations. So there's this nested hierarchy that requires thinking through what gets pushed on.

ARNAIZ It's interesting that from a disciplinary point of view that kind of thinking through nested systems of overlapping hierarchies is perhaps what an architect can bring to the question of the city.

ROWE Yeah. I never think of cities anywhere, it's always in terms of chunks, because that's what I think urban designers do. Urban design has got to do with the materialization of that. And we need to think about and have languages that have got to do with chunks and how they as it were relate to each other. Hierarchically, nonhierarchically, self-similarly, non-self-similarly.

ARNAIZ And that you can puncture into the chunks and make another space. The metaphor of the Russian doll, nested higher levels and scale.

ROWE Right. Nested hierarchies. Frankly, I think it's in the service of facilitation of some social model.

ARNAIZ What do you mean?

ROWE Well, in the Chinese traditional model, the doctrine of li, i.e., proprietary behavior and polite behavior between people, was very prized. In many ways you can see the courtyard house as a facilitation of that, nothing more: insofar as if it faced south, it follows after Confucius saying the sage faced south and pronounced judgment. It also makes a lot of sense with respect to insulation. Fêng shui and pragmatism. The southeast corner is where the gate to welcome the people is and where the sun rises. It's got to do with the introduction to the world, introduction to the day. There's a gate there where you can tie up your horse where a person receives you. Takes you into the lotus court, then leads you out, or you may not even get out of the lotus court, because you're not coming to really visit the family, and then you make your way back through a hierarchy of spaces, et cetera. So the relationship of the space, the arcades, the pavilions, and everything like that is a facilitation of a particular social model. Not an American one. I would say the same thing is true in Colombia. If you asked me, "How would you make housing in Colombia different from, say, the USA?" I'd say, "Well, Colombian society expects what?" A, they're more formal than we are in lots of situations. So the whole vestibule aspect, the whole entry sequence, the presentation of one of these things to the world becomes very important. Also, the Americans, we're much more informal about that, whereas in Colombian society that's more likely to be much more ritualized and as it were semiremote. The private garden circumstance in America, it's not tremendously different from what we call public, whereas here it would be. The only Colombian houses I've ever been in where there were courts and so forth, they were playful. There's a crazy fantasy inside the court, a personal fantasy as juxtaposed against the formality. So the delta between the two is much higher than you get in the American circumstance.

ARNAIZ So true; they're able to dream outlandish fantasies on the inside.

ROWE Yeah. And I think when we come back to this thinking in 3-D in urban design terms, and the nested-hierarchy Russian-doll model, you've got to say, "OK, what could drive that?" I would say facilitation of social propriety and graces. Flexibilities in expectations. That's where you manage the expectations; the magic is in the way you put that together. One key indicator of that is if you go to the informal sectors, they provide them with a box. Then what they do after that, which is oftentimes just, like, rampantly extraordinary, OK, fine, it's lovely. Facilitating a dream. I mean otherwise I think we reduce the whole question of habitation to something that's very functional, very pragmatic, whereas it shouldn't be. Should be deeply fantastic, spiritual, quirky, or at least have the space for that. Otherwise how on earth does religion, philosophy, and so forth inform life? Which it clearly does. These are morals and they have nothing to do with pragmatics usually. As it turns out, in the Chinese example, fêng shui happens to be a set of principles that has a lot of practical aspects to recommend it. Even if you weren't Chinese you'd probably do it that way. But it's not the way it's dressed up. It's a cosmological interpretation of the world. And the self-similarity comes from the first emperor who united China and said, "All under heaven." And he meant it, all under heaven, everybody, me, everybody, under one.

ARNAIZ You think that the model, the idea, of self-similarity is different in different cultures?

ROWE Oh yeah.

ARNAIZ How do you define that?

ROWE Well, China is very direct. If you look at the Forbidden City and its characteristics, the halls and so forth, and you go into Beijing, it's one to one to one to one. But the big hall is an exaggeration of the pavilion at the end of the court. It's quite teeny. Nothing much changes except the scale.

ARNAIZ So the ratio is much more direct.

ROWE Yeah, and you don't have special buildings. Well, with the exception of probably pagodas, but that's because it's obeying another as it were cosmic model. But in the West we're very used to public buildings looking like public buildings. We get very confused when we have buildings that look like public buildings that aren't public buildings. That's how we make sense out of our cities. We have public buildings, buildings that look like what they are. A Gothic cathedral does not look like what? It looks like a particular interpretation of our relationship to God and heaven. We're both Catholics. Yeah, we understand that immediately. But to somebody who's not Christian, it's like, I don't know what the fuck this is about. Dionysius the Areopagite. Give me a break. Who the hell was he? I thought he was a Greek.

ARNAIZ So do you think self-similarity, in this exploded vast open terrain of design today, is still possible?

ROWE Up to a point. I think this is where you make judgment calls. I think self-similarity that then renders public buildings as if they were my mom and dad's house is ridiculous. Doesn't make sense, because our model of the world or our democracy or the government or the institutional framework in which we live doesn't say anything about that. In fact it wants the distinction. So it's a matter of matching all those. The point being, though, that you can think about it in terms of self-similarity or the absence of it or various modulations of that in the way in which the bits go together.

ARNAIZ How do you define self-similarity?

ROWE That A is to B and B is to C and therefore C is to A.

ARNAIZ I'm curious about that in terms of the suggestion that infrastructure can facilitate dreaming or that it may facilitate the potential for the social in the city.

ROWE Yeah, think about how carried away we got with the freeways in the '50s. These bloody great big cars with fins and babes with hats. I mean and we were all into it, yeah, it's great. It was a dream that was really wacky and really persistent for a long period of time. Well, for not a long period of time, but very forcibly intensively for a significant period of time, to more or less create the undergirding of most of the American landscape. Now we're trying to back away from it.

ARNAIZ So what dreams are being facilitated by infrastructure today? I'm curious about your thoughts on China's infrastructure, which is being built at such a rapid pace: new train stations, new airports. What is the dream there?

ROWE Facilitation there, I think of connection, particularly in a country which was totally fragmented and disconnected and remote, where one part was very remote from the other. Contrary to popular opinion, China did not have big cities until relatively recently and the connections between them were pretty far.

ARNAIZ So what do you think is happening in the Chinese imaginary regarding these new connections?

ROWE They're fascinated by time much more than space. For example, I got an email this morning from a bunch of people in Hong Kong. They're saying, "Oh gee whiz. That's China time." I know what they mean. It means bloody rapid. That's China time. There's this fascination with time. By the way, time and timekeeping never entered into the Chinese psyche until the 1920s and '30s in Shanghai, and that was it. It's the only place where you had big clocks.

ARNAIZ That was a Western introduction.

ROWE Yeah, I know. Even in Japan during the Meiji Restoration: the Wako Building clock is a replica of Big Ben.

ARNAIZ Really?

ROWE Yeah, because timekeeping was not a thing. The discipline of timekeeping that's so endemic to the way we live is a relatively remote thing in the Chinese circumstance if you go back not very far in history.

ARNAIZ That's fascinating.

ROWE Now, for example, I think time is as important to them as space. They love the idea that you can get from there to there almost instantaneously, and there's a fascination with fairly basic ideas of efficiency. As we very well know there are certain ideas about dx/dt where x is some activity, dt, where rapidity is not very useful. I don't think that's dawned on the Chinese recently.

ARNAIZ It's like if it's rapid it's useful.

ROWE Yeah. If rapid, it's useful, and you see this in projects. They should take another month and really think about it a little bit further. They might get a bit further. But they don't.

ARNAIZ In the Chinese case, what can we learn from the urban patterns being made today?

ROWE I think this has got to do with managing dynamics. I never think of urban planning or urban design as something that's to do with making things that have a specific spatial conformation. We can do it that way but that, it seems to me, belongs to the 19th century and parts of the 20th century. We're at a point now where we manage dynamics. We manage dynamics with respect to certain performatory characteristics. They've got to do with ecology. They've got to do with social equity. Got to do with economic performance. Got to do with comparative advantages. Got to do with all sorts of measures of that sort. And the formalisms that go along are part of a wide net of relations. So the fact that people say, "Well, Hoover was a great planner," et cetera, I say, "I couldn't care less. To me that's irrelevant." It's got nothing to do with city building. Citizens build cities and they do it in a dynamical fashion which is highly interconnected. And therefore the name of the game is managing the dynamics. And it also sits with this discussion we're having of mesoscale, because what are you doing? You're facilitating something. Whatever the model is.

ARNAIZ Could this provide another way of thinking about typology as a tool to read patterns, understand trends, and perhaps even forecast shifts in urban dynamics?

ROWE It's really interesting. If you look at OECD [Organisation for Economic Co-operation and Development] data on household formation, you'll discover that toward the end of the '80s and into the '90s there was a huge turning point toward diversity. It's talking about who lives with whom and all that sort of thing. And even type of family. And it caught a lot of people by surprise. Off a cliff almost. Which means from a housing point of view that diversity of unit types, mixing of use, integration within the city, connection, and so forth becomes hugely important. So it moved past the problem of simply putting roofs over people's heads and mass production and having similar mass-produced notions, now to the point where we're looking at the complete flip of that. Everything needs to be completely different from everything else.

ARNAIZ So the little exceptions became the mosaic that sustains housing in the contemporary city.

ROWE Yeah. And sometimes there are even bigger exceptions than we might think. You might say driven demographically and driven in terms of habituating. There are all sorts of probable explanations for it. Many places it's a question of affluence. I mean if I'm affluent I can choose my own way of living. Diversity would automatically come into play without me making a big thing of it. That's certainly true. The other has also got to do with what else arrived around about then—going into the late '70s into the '80s in many Western countries. The changeover from broad concepts of thought which were oriented toward positivist outcomes to philosophy of differences, which has got to do with dissimilarities. We're talking about self-similarity before but now we're in a society that has much more to do with dissimilarity. Ironically, the landscape urbanism movement is obsessed with continuity and flows. But if you talk to an ecologist, they say, "Hey, that's not really interesting. What's interesting is the disjunctions and distinctions. The ecotones, the ecotopes. That's what we focus on from a science point of view because that's really where the interest lies. That's where the energy is."

ARNAIZ Yeah. In fact, they're looking at the pressures those distinctions place on species and how this affects interactions in an ecosystem.

ROWE If you go back to [Charles] Eliot, for example, what was interesting there was that in his metropolitan plan for Boston, he was fascinated by, and made the argument for the system based on, the local intrinsic peculiarities of places. He felt that the ensemble had to be protected because that was fundamental to the conservation project. Not the similarities. And if you think about it, most conservation activities historical and otherwise have got to do with distinction and distinctive characteristics, not broad similarities. Except with regard to, "Gee, we need to have this particular environment around." Like I'm going to protect the lilong housing of Shanghai. Up to a point that's probably reasonable. But bear in mind that back in 1930 there was something like 300,000 of these units; virtually everybody lived that way. It was the fabric, and the idea of having parts of that preserved is fine. We're doing that by virtue of distinguishing good bits of it and setting it aside for history.

So a lot of these activities we do, like house historic conservation and stuff like that, has got to do with dissimilarities. If you look at the landmarking movement, '78, all these dates tend to line up against broader shifts in the way in which we think about our world, the way in which we conceptualize our place in the world. Back to this notion of broad social models that drive things. And it's these sorts of fluctuations.

ARNAIZ I want to ask you something about dissimilarity and the shift that you're describing in the OECD countries, and how it might relate to developing countries today. The urgent pressure of providing more modular, standardized, immediate solutions to housing still persists, and yet the access to information at a global scale has created a new consciousness about difference. How should one approach this paradox?

ROWE They know more than we did, a lot more. The cost of information has gone down hugely. I mean if you believe a guy like [Simon] Kuznets who's a Nobel laureate in economics, talking about development, nations as they develop, they get to a certain wealth threshold which allows them to start addressing a much broader range of issues. What we're talking about is certain turning points when the society has its wherewithal internally, economically, socially, politically, otherwise, to move from one regime to another. So the deterritorialization that goes on has got to do with the differences that held together the prior regime disappearing and being replaced by other differences. This is the Ferguson turning-point model, which I think is for us very useful in thinking about urban circumstances because you get material manifestations of this. You look at the 19th century because we actually impute that with that, which I think is why the idea of some sort of broad paradigmatic shaping, highly architecturalized idea of the city for me is not very interesting.

ARNAIZ Would you say that this given way is a reading of the city in terms of Colin Rowe's model collage?

ROWE My problem with that collage is that it means that you understand pieces in formal terms and you look at them in relationship to each other by virtue of this formal terminology. I'm not even sure that—I mean, that's a useful way of doing it, I suppose, up to a point, if you say a city is a palimpsest . . . but I mean how much gets thrown out in that? An awful lot, basically.

ARNAIZ All the dynamics.

ROWE Yeah. All the dynamics. The dynamics have got to do with agency and will and so forth. We're in process at Harvard, a few of us anyway, in rethinking elements, which is a thing I invented when I first went to Harvard. How you introduce architects to urban circumstances. Sitting on reviews recently, it dawned on me and a bunch of others that the students need to have a much bigger grip of agencies in their operations.

ARNAIZ In other words, institutions that are behind.

ROWE Yeah. That exist and serve certain functions, have certain balances of power associated with them.

ARNAIZ All, really. As soon as you hit the ground, that is in a way a version or the other side of the coin of the cultural reading. This seems to be a necessary outgrowth from the cultural awakening in the '70s there by enabling architects to enrich their ability to see the city.

ROWE Yes, and it gets too quickly separated, and we say too quickly, "Well, that's about real estate." It's too quickly categorized as having nothing to do with what I do as an architect or designer. I think that's sheer bullshit. Of course it has everything to do with it, actually. Everything to do with it.

ARNAIZ Especially if you're going back to this question of defining urban design as facilitating dreams. The thing you need to be able to understand is the machine that allows dreaming.

ROWE Allows dreaming or limits or is moving. That's a social construct; it's not an institutional construct. It's partly based on other precedents people refer to. I want it to look like that. That's shorthand. It's fairly palpable but it's shorthand. We need to think beyond that, seems to me. That's why I'm saying a lot of it has got to do with managing the dynamics, what's in play now.

ARNAIZ What are some of the big ideas with respect to teaching urban design that are going to shape the future of how the curriculum is written?

ROWE Well, I'm not exactly sure I know yet. You've got to try to sort out what can you actually teach versus what they will just experience through life flowing over them. Some get drowned. Others don't. What can you teach? I think you can teach lessons.

ARNAIZ Case studies?

ROWE Yeah, for example, let's take a big buzzword these days. PPPs. Joint public-private partnerships. Everybody talks about that, whether it's got to do with developing countries, all the way through. What do they actually mean? What actually is a public-private venture? How is it located in a social set of circumstances? And how is it narrowed down or amplified? I think it's a very important thing to get your head around. What drives it and what shapes it. What to look out for. If you're going somewhere and you're going to get involved with PPPs what on earth could it possibly mean? That's something that's very teachable. The issues about infrastructure and infrastructural efficiencies are something that we can do. Resilience. How do you think about urban resilience movement forward through time? If I'm saying it's managing the dynamics ipso facto I'm saying I need to know how possible futures materialize themselves. Therefore, I need to know what are the characteristics of these physical or quasiphysical things, like infrastructure, moving through time. How do they line up against stacks of money? How do they line up against questions of who benefits? A lot of those basic metrics you can devise exercises to do in broad terms.

ARNAIZ What about some of the topics that we've touched on today, such as the question of dissimilarity? This tendency or the need to think of the mesoscale? Nested?

ROWE One of the big issues for me is in urban areas. This goes back to our contextual fascination during the '70s and part of the '80s. How well grounded was that? In my view, way overplayed. We were expecting history in a sense to solve all sorts of problems, which history obviously couldn't, because the underlying conditions had disappeared entirely. So we need to have a critical stance toward this sort of stuff, and ask fundamentally how useful is this typology today and why, before we say, "Well, gee, we're going to keep it." Other than the conservation argument, which says we're keeping it around because we want to have a Noah's Ark at the end of the day. Which has also got critical thinking. Do I need Noah's Arks at the end of the day?

ARNAIZ You could say that resiliency is defined by diversity, making an argument for a living and connected Noah's Ark.

ROWE Yeah, one of the biggest issues given the asset values of communities is how do we move them from, say, state A to state B, where there's a regime shift, in a manner where we don't have to tear everything down. In other words, where the basic form can adapt and be retrofitted. Specialization in time A to specialization in time B requires despecialization if A is different, B is different from A. This is one of the big problems haunting China at the moment. It's not a question of whether they're building badly. The buildings are falling down. They've always been good engineers. Funny thing is, during the Baroque and so forth they rebuilt all the time. They had no problem with that at all. We're wimps these days.

ARNAIZ You talk about the 30-year redundancy of a building in China when it should be 70 to 100 years. Are there things that we can do that actually can flip that 30-year redundancy into a longer life?

ROWE Yeah, and they're trying to do that. Matter of fact, I'm going to be doing a studio next semester in a place called Shekou in Shenzhen. And it's an industrial district—and I don't know much about industry, but I'm going to learn—where they've got very new stuff going on with stuff that's just factories that are just no longer useful. And they're saying, "Well, should we really pull that down, or try to make it into something else?" And they're doing more of the latter.

ARNAIZ The first people to go in.

ROWE How do we do that? We get developers interested in putting a program that allows it to exist along with giving them some benefits to make their money on the side. That's the way the creative district model works in Shanghai and elsewhere in China. It's pretty good really. Sometimes the baby goes out with the bathwater. You end up with tall office buildings next to nice little factories, which doesn't make any sense really. But generally it's a reasonably robust model. We should try to think about ways to reuse stuff if it has some merit, or not.

ARNAIZ One of the interesting things we found, in this project we're doing, involving the reuse of a sugar mill, is that scale and connections of the negatives matter more than the structure. We spent a few weeks and basically found that they work like microcities, foregrounding the void over the object.

ROWE That's right. Tokyo, unfortunately, is used to disappearing every 50 to 100 years. In 1923, blam, earthquake; 1945, the Americans knocked it for six. In 1657 it burned. Oomph. Got to start from zero again. So the whole idea of monument is obviously influenced by catastrophic events where it's not so much the object. For example, Nihonbashi, which was a central figure in a lot of Tokyo, a lot of Japan, refers to the Bridge of Japan, of which there'd been lots of versions. But it's not so much the object. It's the place and the notion of a Nihonbashi that remains. And actually it's a plaque about yea big in the pavement. Because any reasonable expectation beyond that is crazy. It seems to me there are huge distinctions between figural and formal sets of circumstances. If we're talking about objects it's largely figural, and if we're talking about urban circumstances we probably should be more interested in the formal aspect. But of course there is the figure of the form as well. And then there's the form of the figure. The games like that get intertwined. But I think we should be fairly clear. If it's in formal terms we're interested in the typology of things. We're interested in certain key aspects of geometry. We're not necessarily that interested in the immediate historic or expressive aspect of things, it seems to me. And that's a useful way to move forward. So in thinking as you were doing—I think it was correct to say, "Well, rather than talking about the sheds as such, maybe a few sheds are worth paying some attention to; we need to think about how they were arranged, how much of that makes sense now."

ARNAIZ I just recently got a call from someone in the Philippine government to be part of a team to aid in the rebuilding of communities devastated by Typhoon Haiyan. How should we rebuild? How much or little monumentality? When you brought up this question of Nihonbashi my reaction was that we should be thinking much more about arrangement. Much more about the kind of formal organization of the thing, as opposed to the figural planting of certain pieces that can provide.

ROWE If we think of Tokyo, there's very little vestige when you go there of the pre-Meiji shogunate period. Very little vestige in expressive terms. On the other hand, formally speaking, there's huge—it hasn't really moved at all. It manifests itself very very differently.

ARNAIZ Why does Tokyo seem at first so surreal to an outsider?

ROWE It's culturally enormously distinct even though everything was built yesterday. But it's culturally enormously distinct because it has this formal underlying palimpsest quality that is inescapable. It doesn't exist anywhere else. It's not canonical form in the Sino-Japanese Korean way. It's not that at all. It's not Kyoto. Kyoto is emulating the "Kaogongji" of the Zhouli, the canonical form of the Chinese capitals. There's none of that. But Tokyo is like no other place on earth, even when you get out in the burbs where it's essentially suburban, going back to this business about private yards. They're little, dinky. And the density is very high. I'm doing this book where we're looking at urban intensity. One of the aspects of this is density. If you take, for example, House NA in Sendagaya-ku, or you take the teardrop house, they're very small, but if you think of them in aggregate terms they have a density of about 100 persons per hectare. They're single houses. It's phenomenal.

ARNAIZ This distinction that you just made between the figural and the formal, especially in terms of Tokyo's empty non-monumental center surrounded by the moat of daimyo estates with the fabric of the Meiji period beyond supporting the emergence of a hi-tech city, is a fascinating urban model.

ROWE The other aspect of the figural and formal is that if you look at something like the *Yingzao Fashi*, which was a building code, a manual, it's a staggering thing, it's like this deep. It was written in the 12th century during the Song dynasty when one of the emperors there or one of the major power brokers decided that we have a problem. Stuff is burning down. It's unsafe. People are getting ripped off with respect to money on construction, due to rampant corruption in the construction industry. So he turns to this guy Li and he says, "Listen, buddy. This is the issue." So Li goes away and he comes up with the Yingzao Fashi, which is a building code, where it's based on a module where you can relate that to cost. So for any building, no matter what, you can come up with a bill of quantities and you can say, "Listen," to the carpenter, "it needs to get close to this or else I'm going to put you in jail." And also it's done in such a way that it's not going to fall down or burn indiscriminately.

ARNAIZ Wasn't there another manual concerned with means?

ROWE Yes, it couldn't care less about the ends. So it's got to do with process of buildings, ends, it's means. It's not ontological; it's teleological in its orientation. Then it goes back to what's the purpose of architecture. Facilitate righteous proprietous behavior. I'm fully convinced that to understand traditional Chinese architecture and urbanism you have to think of it as means, not ends. Even though the ends are quite beautiful and wonderful.

ARNAIZ Doesn't this get us back to the question of managing dynamics?

ROWE Yes. The Qianlong emperor and the emperor during the Song I don't think was enormously concerned with the aesthetics of some artifact. He was immensely concerned with developing a process whereby the city could exist. So he was managing the dynamics from that perspective, not in terms of some preconceived architecturalized planimetric expression. That's where I part company with people who want to see urban design solely in those terms. Yeah, I can think of it expressively.

ARNAIZ Managing the dynamics. Facilitating dreams. There we go.

ROWE That's what it's about, really.

ARNAIZ Peter, thank you so much.

—Recorded December 13, 2013

DUKS KOSCHITZ,

PHIL PARKER,

AND

CARLOS ARNAIZ

ARNAIZ Form seems to me to insist less on a particular kind of rational organization than geometry might. Even if you decide to avoid it, in geometry, it's very clear when you are breaking from some kind of order or when you pursue a set of rules. Form doesn't seem to have that kind of history.

PARKER Are you saying geometry is breaking from the rules?

ARNAIZ No, that geometry has that tradition. It has that history. It has the ghost of a system, the shadow there, all the time. Whether you acknowledge it or not, it's there. One of the reasons that we are drawn to geometry is that it relates to certain building systems. It relates to assembly methods. It relates to a particular way of bringing a project together. For example, in the Hue Hotel, we were playing around with form—different versions of the bean—and then realized, well, how are we really going to communicate this to the contractor? This is not a very sophisticated place for building. We can't rely on highly digitized forms of construction with factory-made panels that come in with a particular level of rigor. And at that point, geometry all of a sudden played a very significant role as a kind of ordering system. We realized that there were only three or four points on the plan that we knew and from that, we built a gridded system through which they could locate the curve in this classical way of building a curve geometry based on a series of points.

PARKER So plot the discrete points?

ARNAIZ Yeah, that's right, and everything emanated out of that. That became, in a way, the guiding principle. I think that's an interesting difference between form and geometry. Because geometry is the organizing system. I think that's why the question of, also, how much does it police intuition, to me, is interesting.

PARKER The reason I'm asking is because the second you draw anything as geometry, it's made. Because every shape that you can draw is one description, one representation of geometry. And it sounds like, to you, geometry has to do with a rational operation—the post-rationalization of a shape—where that description may, in that process, lead to a description that is different than it was at the beginning, and that is what you might call restricting. So, post-rationalization—that's an issue?

ARNAIZ I have an issue with that term.

PARKER The "post"?

ARNAIZ Well, "rationalization"; what about execution? Yes, it's true that there is a shape or a geometrical reference point which any shape has, but the fact is that we're dealing with coordination of different systems, communication with different individuals, in the execution of any built structure. Geometry is not so much post-rationalization as it is a tool, an instrument to work through the issue of materializing shapes at multiple scales.

PARKER But there you're trying to find even the appropriate system of measure, in terms of geometry. One set of measures I can use when I'm making a sketch. There's another one when I'm working on the computer. And there's another one when I'm in the construction field, in the practice. But in the terms we're talking about here, it's interesting that they're all really built out of a two-dimensional field. So it's plane geometry, extruded or projected from a plane surface, as distinct from working in multi-dimensional symmetries or something like that. So you're working out of a plane, in most of the terms, which can make a lot of sense. Like you said, it began with a layout and the curve. Geometry seems to—certainly historically, in terms of Euclid—probably start with the two-dimensionality of the plane. So, the plane is already demanding a "geometry."

ARNAIZ Well, that's interesting, because, I mean, maybe then the question is, is the studio's idea of geometry prefigured or contained by a specific idea of drawing?

KOSCHITZ I think you have an image in your head when you say "geometry."

ARNAIZ I don't know. I mean, that's part of this conversation. (laughter)

KOSCHITZ Just the use of the word.

ARNAIZ OK.

KOSCHITZ Right? So, what is the aesthetics of geometry? But the answer should be, geometry is a subset in math. It describes anything. And so, it has any aesthetic. So, geometry can't have aesthetics. It only can have aesthetics if you think it has the potential for beauty. That's a value judgment. And then, I would argue that we should be talking about form in architecture, not geometry. And then we can talk about the cultural implications of form, or form in architecture, as whatever critical practice or commercial. I would like to know how you define geometry for this conversation.

ARNAIZ Well, to be honest with you, we're not sure. The process by which we got to that word was that we looked through the projects and tried to extract a few concepts around which we are organizing these conversations. So, last week we had a conversation on urbanism. And next week, I'm having a conversation on the diagram. Now, are those really the right concepts? I'm not really sure. I think what's at stake here are issues of drawing; issues of projection; issues of assembly and construction; issues of practice. So, again, geometry right now is a kind of stand-in. Maybe it's misleading. I am interested in this question of the aesthetics in geometry. What do you think, Phil, about that statement?

PARKER It's a little bit like saying what's the aesthetics of calculus?

KOSCHITZ Now, that's one geometry. It's a bit overstated, but then there's Terry Winters here, who in one way or another deals with geometry. If you go through his work, part of the issue is the ways in which the line has been redeployed, so to speak. That's actually quite an interesting piece.

PARKER The line is a territory I know a fair amount of. Is there an aesthetic to English or something? Is it a question of form, or is it a question of measure? Is it a question of relation? All of those parts become subsets of concepts of beauty, or ways in which it ends up getting broken down. Each one of your terms, intuition, novelty, means of production, efficiency, aesthetic, simplicity, seems to be searching for something you can use that would link them together. Do you go from novelty to efficient or inefficient production through use of geometry? OK, so, what are your interests in intuition, novelty, production? What drives a project, and so forth? I would say it's not geometry. I don't think geometry does almost any of the things, in terms of what disciplines intuition. I think intuition is what disciplines itself. An intuition is a complex thing. It's not the casual, you know, "I walk this way." That's not intuitive. Intuition is, "When do I walk when I can no longer walk? When do I speak when I can only . . . ?"It's what you rub up against when push comes to shove. So, it's not the measure. It's not the rationality. It's something else, I think. But can it produce novelty? Not by itself. It has to have a driver. Someone has to do it. Can it exist outside of the means of production? Well, it probably always does, right? (laughter)

ARNAIZ Let's take the scripting world. It's geometrical units and objects that are manipulated via a script. Yes, there was something novel to it, because the tools became available, and everybody started experimenting. Perhaps this is how one describes "novelty"; you could say the spline in architecture led to blobitecture. And so the definition of this curve and its accessibility through software has changed the language of architecture. But it's hard to blame the representation of the curve. The curve became available in software. The software became available to designers. And designers started to play with it, and then they just liked it, fell in love with it, and did it. So the novelty is a mixture of serendipity and romance. There is actually nothing novel about scripting, per se. [Leon Battista] Alberti did that, in terms of a specification of form, and how to verbalize a geometric description rather than doing it through drawing. That's a very old idea.

PARKER But Alberti set out the terms that said this is architecture. (laughs) And then, scripting, or the use of the spline, or other techniques of manipulating a fundamental unit in geometry—the line—is, I argue, the kind of well-formulated legacy of what the architect is to do to lay out the lines. That's the end of the job.

ARNAIZ Or the beginning.

PARKER Yeah. (laughter) But it's interesting that it's not geometry, right? It's a different level of instruction or specification, in a way, that the line does. It is absolutely embedded in geometry, but it is not the same as geometry.

KOSCHITZ It's very much about representation in math and in architecture. That's why I was suggesting that we just replace *geometry* with *form*. That is where the cultural and the semantic aspect of it starts to kick in. For instance, how does geometry drive a project? How does your understanding of geometry or your love of a certain type of shape and its geometric description drive a project? If you like triangles and you want to do something with triangles, then triangles can drive a project.

ARNAIZ One reason why I find form less interesting than geometry goes back to the way you described architecture as laying out the line, which is such a wonderful phrase. Because *form*, to me, implies a particular completeness. But we're talking about forms and shapes. It seems to have less ability to break itself into its analytical components than the word *geometry* does. For example, take the idea of a triangle. One reason why I would like to think geometry as method, as opposed to forms of the triangle, is that, using a kind of geometric outlook, we can ask questions about the triangle about the angles of the triangle; legs; arms; how the triangle is put together; whether we have different types of triangles. That, to me, opens up the possibility of interrogating form. Do you break the triangle? At some point after this type of geometric interrogation, you decide that the triangle might not work as you commonly define it. That might be the breakthrough. If you start with a particular formal definition of a triangle, it is not easy to unravel the triangle. I'm interested in the geometric limits and the potential for the triangle to go beyond itself through an understanding that is based on three lines and three angles. The line seems to propose a systemic approach to the field, as opposed to a formal approach that determines that we're dealing with triangles or circles.

PARKER I mean, the problem for me is one of process. In the beginning, when you talk about novelty and means of production then the geometry seems to have a kind of passive reception rather than form, which is understood as being somehow involved in formation and informing.

ARNAIZ Yes.

PARKER So, it's actually involved in the process of production, as distinct from being the thing produced. There is some way in which those things, if you start to unpack it, arrive or become deformed. I think more contemporaneously, more in terms of form and matter, there's a difference between shape, which is perhaps closer to geometry as already related to two dimensions, and form.

ARNAIZ Yeah, I would agree. Form is about how shapes culturally communicate.

PARKER And how they're engendered—how they're produced—how they arrive. I mean, it gives you a larger repertoire. Form slides a lot more between an organic and an inorganic, and you don't have to deal with those terms anymore. It gives us a way of thinking about the ways in which things come into being, if you will.

KOSCHITZ I'll give you an example of how I like to think about these things. If you have three points and you connect those with line segments, you have the coordinates of these three. So you have a location, and you can, then, define the line segments. This is the most conducive way of defining what a triangle is, in computer science, because you're doing it through location. Let's say you can define a triangle through the three angles in the three corners. But you will always think of these as a rigorous geometric description of elements coming together. So, it's a rigorous description of shapes. It's strongly rooted in math. But it's not really geometry. And that's sort of an in-between way, and I like your distinction, to say you can go from geometry to shape and form. Because in architecture, I do think form means a lot more than shape does. For argument's sake, we can say, all right, let's just replace it with shape. How does shape drive a project? OK, so you could say, well, you'll have your own handwriting. You like tetrahedra, and you like the shape of it, and you usually like to replace one of the solid sides with something transparent. And so you can say that that's a root of a project. But the rigorous description of it doesn't really help.

ARNAIZ I find the concept of a "rigorous description" of a form interesting, because it seems to me that the method by which you choose to describe the form affects the evolution of the form. I remember thinking a lot about FOA's [Foreign Office Architects] Yokohama Terminal while I was a student, as it has this evolutionary intelligence when it went from competition entry into built form precisely because of the geometric tools that they chose to use to describe it to the builders. So the form evolved, changed and came into being differently at each stage, yet retained a conceptual consistency because of a rigorous geometric description of form.

KOSCHITZ I would argue that that was the big failure of the project. It's not what FOA wanted. They wanted the smooth, blobby project, and they got a triangulated—

ARNAIZ I don't really care what they wanted. Let's leave the architect's intent behind.

KOSCHITZ The project itself is a great project.

ARNAIZ If you arrived from Mars, and you found the competition drawings, and you visited the project that gap is fascinating. Who cares what Alejandro [Zaera-Polo] and Farshid [Moussavi] really did there?

KOSCHITZ If I know the competition entry, in my book, it's a failure.

ARNAIZ Really?

KOSCHITZ Yeah. It's like they're bad architects. If you don't know how to handle a NURB in building, then you shouldn't do it, and just start with triangles from the get-go. Get an understanding of polygons and meshes and then I want to see mesh studies. Then I want to see exactly which polygons are being investigated, and how and why and where. And not that sort of low-resolution proposal, you know, which sort of inevitably happened because they were inexperienced.

ARNAIZ But that's what got them to win. It was that kind of dreamy, blurry landscape, right? I mean, give me a break. Thirty? And you're doing a project in three weeks; are you really going to do 25,000 mesh studies? What you're doing is communicating and channeling a dream, right?

KOSCHITZ But that's a different conversation.

ARNAIZ But that's the reality of it. That's why I think what's quite fascinating is how geometry figures into the reality of practice.

PARKER Well, there are two different geometries. There's a design geometry and a kind of rendered geometry. There's a rendered image, and a set of construction practices, where they have to be rationalized. So the two things are brought together, which brings us to the question of which one comes first. In other words, do you develop the means of production, which then gives you the possibility of making a rendering, which is going to be different when you make the rendering, and then figure out how to produce it? We know very well that they both are running, you know, constantly, in anyone's practice.

ARNAIZ Yeah, and they're both informing themselves. In other words, you do the rendering and then you figure out how to produce it. It's constant mutation based on your ability to describe it. It's almost post-structuralist in that the means by which we interpret the world will shape our world. And the means that we have to read our form is geometry. So the tool that we use will inform the kind of possible decisions we take, or even the kind of possible transformations that it engenders as it moves forward.

PARKER Is geometry a tool? That's the hard part for me. Because to me it's a component of a tool. It's the handle or the weight. It's not the tool. Tool is a much larger constellation—the software, and those bits of geometry that's involved, and the sort of history of the tool. It's the fuller constellation of the apparatus of producing a design, and ultimately producing a building. And it's a larger set of constraints that go into the production. Well, I guess that's our problem as architects, is that we tend to think we can turn the tool into something that's not a tool. (laughter) The tool is a much larger constellation of ways in which that device has been implemented and used in the implementation of things over a much longer history.

KOSCHITZ I'm not going to let that one sit.

ARNAIZ Please don't. This is the point of this conversation.

KOSCHITZ I really do think the Yokohama project is a wonderful project in telling architects that they need to do their homework, in terms of understanding geometry. So if you are too, excuse the word, stupid to figure out how to build a NURB, then you haven't done your homework. I don't like the practice of mystification in competitions. I find that fundamentally boring, because it's always the same story. "Yeah, we had this great dream, and it was this fantastic project." And then, you know, the client didn't have the money, or the client didn't have the time, or whatever. "People didn't like it because we were so radical." Bullshit. Provide an image of something that is buildable. Provide the vision through the right means.

ARNAIZ But there's another conversation; competitions actually beg for that type of an approach.

PARKER I think there is a place where—and it's part of the utopian dream, right? You're putting something out, way ahead of your knowledge base. And you're going, OK, this is where I'm going to head. And I don't really know how I'm going to get there, but I feel like it's going to work in these ways. And so I don't think that's out of place. I think it's certainly fully within—inside of—architecture. In fact, if we could only propose what we can build—what we already know how to build—then we couldn't act, right?

KOSCHITZ Yeah, I would agree. There's a place for speculation everywhere. There's plenty of room and place for that kind of exploration, and I'm in full favor of it. But in terms of this very project, there was a dream. And the project is, compared to the dream, crap. And it's because of the misunderstanding of which geometric representation works for construction. It's very simple. And so I think the disappointment of the executed project is a problem, but this is competition culture, which we shouldn't talk about.

PARKER I can give you a different image. As a very young undergraduate student—this has to be off the record or something.

ARNAIZ Oh, no, this is all on the record.

PARKER I know, I know. It's so ancient, but it's this beautiful little image that Le Corbusier made of a watch case, which, if I have it correctly in my head, is a little bumblebee and a kind of geometrical pattern. You know, shifted planes that are sliding like that, right?

ARNAIZ Can you draw it?

PARKER You know, it was like this. Something like a bumblebee sitting on a flower. So, in something like that, he stated a geometrical problem. He was 14 or something when he did that. So, there's this watch case. And it sets out his predicament, which he died with, and which is between those two forms of measurement, right?

ARNAIZ The bumblebee versus the . . . ?

PARKER Call it the grid.

ARNAIZ The grid.

PARKER Yeah, what became a skyline.

ARNAIZ Skyline, but it's some kind of, like, matrix of lines on a grid?

PARKER Yes.

ARNAIZ Interesting.

PARKER Yeah, they were engraved in the watch case. But the point I'm getting at is the issue of stating—using formative principles—he draws the planes differently, and the bee. Or they have, in his view, at that time, certainly two very different origins, because he made that distinction, the natural and the—geometric. So, it stated that kind of thing. And in another way, maybe, Yokohama states the opposite—that these things are fused. And this sort of ocean-liner building is all fused in a kind of geometry—a form of measure. So, it's a different statement.

ARNAIZ Yeah, absolutely.

PARKER And a different way of working with those geometrical orders. That was quite powerful, even while accepting its bizarre geometries. But I think part of the question is how one uses various forms of organization to set up the predicament, the questions of the day, of the time. I'm still fascinated by the resolution or irresolution of the base, and whether it's coming through, and the tower with the curved piece. And then, how that moves into the glass and glazing structure, and how it moves down into the other thing. A place where, it seems to me, the geometrical order, the formal order (laughs), in that sense, or the way in which the form was made, can be even more concretely addressed.

ARNAIZ The Corbusier story, of the grid and the bee, versus the Yokohama? I think it's an interesting pairing. Certainly this one speaks to the sort of modernist obsession with opposites. And the Yokohama struggles to be a kind of hybrid where in the lumps and inconsistencies are representations of our half-bred condition. One of my favorite pieces of that project is the glass façade in which they were trying to eliminate the structural glass fins and arrived at this strange, in-between, large-scale corrugated-glass surface that is neither here nor there. That's actually quite compelling, perhaps, as a statement of where we are in the dream, or in the nightmare, of modernity, we obsess over distinctions yet produce hybrids. Our reality is bumpier and this Frankenstein is a beautiful homage to our incomplete present.

KOSCHITZ If you look at the development of all of Frank Gehry's work, he's got, intuitively, the right geometric description in mind. Sure, you can tell me that everything that Frank Gehry drew was something that we knew because you could make it out of a piece of paper. But I find there is a lot more to learn there than in the, "Oh, I'm going to make a papier-mâché model for a competition, and then I figured out that I had to make it in I-beams." So there's a frustration for a real project. What I very much liked was, Phil, when you started to describe the nature of a tool. So, there are many productive ways of thinking of how to control shapes, which I think is how you are thinking of geometry. There are certain proportions and elements that need to be there for it to be an archetype. And then, you investigate iterations and you're trying to distort it to the point where maybe the type gets dissolved. And you can do that, visually, very easily. You can do that with just following—you need to set up what the archetype is, in terms of proportions, maybe angles, sizes, that kind of thing. And then you can just play. If you think of the word *algorithm* as the rules that define how things are related to one another, an algorithm is a rule set that you're going through. That's one way, maybe, to think of a more practical definition or description that you can build. It's a parametric definition based on relational geometry, which is very powerful. I mean, the Greeks started that. It's very old math, because you're working in proportions to one another, so it's less of a numeric game. Which is very useful when you're using archetypes, and trying to alter them.

ARNAIZ I'm curious about your understanding of Frank Gehry. You seem to be saying you find it, as a form of architectural research, let's say, more coherent than what was produced in Yokohama. Is that correct?

KOSCHITZ If I look at the first sketches of Disney Hall, and I look at the final project, I'm not frustrated.

PARKER But Gehry does a certain thing, though. He buys himself an incredible amount of room by the way he operates skin and structure. And so he says exactly, "Yes, you can make it of paper. And I can structure this thin membrane, whether it's stone or metal or any sort, because I'm building something behind it." And Yokohama didn't actually make that distinction between structure and surface, enclosure, and so forth. And by merging all of that together, then there's another set of constraints that Gehry is very smart, in terms of his maintenance of certain incredibly important modernist operations—

ARNAIZ Correct.

PARKER Separate structure and enclosure, and program, really. I mean, it's like, OK, just take care of it.

ARNAIZ Yeah, which is why I found your term "inconsistency" interesting. Because, to me, part of what makes Gehry so fascinating is his ability to stomach so much inconsistency, and to, in fact, push those systems that were already somewhat separate in modernism even farther away from each other. While Yokohama is an aspirational stab toward complete consistency.

PARKER Well, Gehry is a collagist at heart.

ARNAIZ And it fails, in your mind, because it's not completely consistent.

PARKER Well, the surface isn't even structural. It doesn't have to be.

KOSCHITZ It's like all the promises are out the window.
ARNAIZ You're right. Exactly. Did you fall in love with that, or do you belong to the camp that wants that promise?

KOSCHITZ So, Zaha [Hadid]'s fire station was not a frustration. If you look at her very first oil paintings, it's all in the building, and it's all consistent, and it's all there. You know, and she fought the right battles, in my opinion.

PARKER See, I think Gehry gains a lot of strength from working off of typologies, or working off set pieces that are distorted. Especially the concert hall's relation to Los Angeles. You can see the difference if you compare the concert hall with his Experience Music Project in Seattle; the latter has nothing to work against and the distortions are less located. Where do you locate your geometry, if you will, in your terms? How do you work with different geometries? I think there's a very big difference between working with boundary borders versus internal grain.

ARNAIZ Fascinating point! I'm trying to relate profile and grain to some of the terms we've been using earlier in the conversation, such as shape and system or shape and measure. Is profile analogous to shape? Measure is closer to grain? Perhaps grain is the kind of particulate matter that is unitized, striated and repeated, and that can have a gradient of densification across the field so that depending on how that system of measurement is deployed, it hopefully affects the kind of overall shape. I painted it as a linear progression from one to the other.

PARKER Right, or as a hierarchy. But in the fish trap, or the hat, that's not the way it works.

ARNAIZ Yeah, that's not the case.

PARKER The form is much more integrally related to the local order of the line.

ARNAIZ Correct.

PARKER That's sort of what it comes to. (laughs) That's why you're saying it's geometry, because you're actually articulating it consistently with this one unit, the line.

ARNAIZ Mm-hmm. If Corbusier's geometric problem is the bee and the grid, maybe in our work, the unresolved relationship between the profile and the grain might be the conundrum we're struggling with.

KOSCHITZ If you look at the first version of the Hue Hotel you have two splines on top of one another. So I assume that the motivation to work with an extrusion has to do with, you know, economic pressures. You can focus on a profile in one direction, but not in the other.

ARNAIZ Yes. Economic pressures pretty much start all projects. Most of our projects are in the developing world. All of our projects have incredibly short timelines. All of our projects have extremely tight budgets.

KOSCHITZ And so, if economics determine a certain kind of form, I would say, then you try to set up something where you can still play. So, all right, if I can do extrusion, I can do one profile, and I can find a way to describe this spline to the contractors. Well, then, we can put two on top of one another that are not the same. And that is, obviously, more interesting than a two-story extrusion, I would say. And I think that's consistent in all projects. You know what it is that you can afford, and then set up the game, and try to play as much as you can.

ARNAIZ Yeah, that was the 100 Walls situation. We knew how many seats we had to have. We knew how big it had to be. We knew what the budget would be. We knew that half the budget would actually go into the formation—making sure that this was flood resistant, because it's on reclaimed land right next to the water, in a place in the world where you have storm surges and monsoons. And so, what can we build with the rest of the money? Well, a hundred different walls, because labor is inexpensive. And to build a hundred different walls in a hundred different shapes is a material reality that was both compelling and doable. OK, so do that. I mean, is that sometimes dumb, really?

KOSCHITZ Well, it's not dumb. It's the opposite. I think it's intelligent, because you identified the available means, and then played with those. So it's a game with constraints. The only thing that's dumb is the individual wall, not what you are doing with it.

PARKER I agree with that. It wouldn't be dumb at all. I do have a question about that. I'm curious as to what other patterns are part of that directionality? It could have been five degrees this way, or 200 degrees that way, to look at it. I don't know. So, I was really curious as to what actually established the directionality of the grain. Because it's a grain this way, and a processional that way, right? They're perpendicular to one another. And they have light issues, wind, maybe tidal flow—hopefully not. (laughs) Air at high speed, and typhoons or something. There are a lot of potential linkages that I was curious about, as to what organized those.

ARNAIZ The first operation was to establish the north-south, east-west relationship for the sunset. After that, there was a social-political question related to the access. Part of the idea of the hundred walls was to disguise the door. We had a problem with the door. There is a prevailing notion in churches that the first thing you see is the door. Yet we wanted you to actually get lost. We had this idea that the walls were like the gardens of Gethsemane for Christ, the one place in the world where he's actually lost, and where he finds God. And so we wanted to work with disorientation. Convincing the priests and clients of that idea was actually quite challenging.

PARKER I could imagine. (laughter)

ARNAIZ And so that was one of the struggles, how deeply embedded can you put the door, so that you don't find it, and you don't find the main access. And I would say it ended up being a compromise.

PARKER But that goes to one of your questions about access and so forth, and the blockage, and the passage. That's actually a very powerful thing, I think, where a geometric logic is interrupted by a culture's desire for passage. The imposition, or the logic of one order—the procession—is countered by the other one, or delayed. It's not blocked. You do get in. It's not like you can't get there from here. You do get in, it's just delayed. So the unit is used to produce a double, right? One is the space of loss, and the other is the recapture, or the enlightenment. I mean, this is like this magical moment when you pass through the threshold. Otherwise, the church is known for being able to see the big gate. You see the opening first, to get in, right? (laughs)

ARNAIZ Right, yeah. A friend who is a theologian, at some point before the construction of the church, saw the plan, and made this comment about the Gothic versus the rational church. And said that, in the Gothic model of the relationship to God, there was a lot of mystery. We don't really know who he or she is. But with the Enlightenment, there was a sort of the sense of clarity introduced by sciences that in fact he is embodied in us. This results in an architectural directness in churches after the Enlightenment. And to some degree his comment was the 100 Walls is much more in the Gothic tradition—the delay you're talking about produces a "what is this thing?" effect.

PARKER There's also the geometry of mazes. It can be used as a way in which an image of loss, or "chaos," can be produced. But it's deliberately amorphous, right?

ARNAIZ Yeah. Deliberately trying to do away with a specific form of the thing through the repetition of a line.

—Recorded December 16, 2013

AMY WHITAKER

AND

CARLOS ARNAIZ

WHITAKER So I teach product designers a business structures class. And so I think about how information gets distributed in flat surfaces, often, or in small, domestic-scale objects. And I was thinking about signage as a starting point and how a lot of the purpose of communication of signage is to create a shorthand, a visual shorthand. And I think one of the reasons that you create a shorthand is that it allows people to quickly orient themselves, and that scales up into architecture in a way that has to do with the ability to be autonomous in a public space, the ability, essentially, to spatially be a citizen. And some of that relates to my interest in museums, that I want people to have an independent-thinking, personal-creativity relationship to the public library part of museums. But in this case, I'm really curious about how you think, when you are designing master plans or public spaces—how you think about the experience of the person learning how to navigate the space as an act of communication.

ARNAIZ Looking at some of our work and thinking through your phrase "to spatially be a citizen" makes me retrospectively theorize this as an aspiration of ours. There's a lot of work that falls under the category of urbanism where we're designing districts and neighborhoods. So this question of how do you know where you are, how do you place this locale in the context of adjacent places in the city, and the overall question of orientation in a condition of relative disorientation is extremely prescient.

WHITAKER Right.

ARNAIZ In fact, in many of the cities that we operate in, which are in the developing world, we have a fascinating and complex relation to order. Manila, for example, has a chaotic overlapping history stemming from colonialism, war, dictatorships, and lack of any municipal framework operating on the entire urban territory. In a city like New York, you have a gridded plan, with continuous street signs, sidewalks and bike paths. One of the things you become most aware of in these developing cities is the power of the private sector. The result is a de facto fragmentation. There is continuity in public space in one zone, then—poof!—it vanishes when you leave the developer's domain. The overall effect is a mosaic of different orders and different publics. I think the problematic that these cities brings up is that, if the challenge is to spatially be a citizen, that notion of citizenship in this kind of context has to be more adaptable to the reality of this kind of overlapping histories without a clear identity.

WHITAKER It's really interesting, and also humbling, what you're saying about the overlapping histories of Manila. Because a lot of the autonomy of navigation of space by an individual is a democratic concept. Which is perhaps, in a benign way, related to autocratically planned Western cities, which are dependent on a unified voice that can set a system. I think it's really fascinating what you're saying about Manila, that you're maybe not orienting people to be autonomous citizens but autonomous explorers. Because they have to be able to go from one area to another. And I'm curious what it must be like for you to participate as an individual voice or an individual actor and as a firm, in a space in relation to the, sort of, chaos.

The way I think of orientation and access is from the museum side. I used to love the old Museum of Modern Art building, more than I realized I did until they built the new one. One of the things that I miss is that you used to be able to walk in and immediately orient yourselves, because there were these long escalators that faced the gardens. You always knew where you were in space. You could disappear into the depths of the gallery but you could always come back to the escalator. And now the escalator is hidden in the inside of the building. And it's at an individual rather than public scale. You can't pass people on it. And the Tate Modern, similarly, has these vast escalators that keep you relatively oriented. The windows to the outside and the escalator keep you oriented. So you always know where those are. And then many of the galleries have windows onto the Thames and to St. Paul's, across the river. So there's some way in which you see where you are. And I'm really curious how you think about that when you tackle an individual project, because there's less control of the space or you're reacting more to a chaos that's long-standing, and how you make decisions in that area, how you let people know the signals of what the building is and how to interact with it and what's asked of them when they walk into it, and how much they're asking for that kind of orientation or autonomy and how much they're asking for something else.

ARNAIZ Three terms came to mind when you asked that question. Three concepts that we use a lot in the office: One is legibility. The other one is repetition. And the last would be scale. And how much legibility can we imbue—without being autocratic, without it being pedantic or heavy? How often do you repeat something without it being monotonous while still creating the sense of mnemonic register? What's the right scale? It's funny that you bring up the MoMA. We have an urban project that measures about 3.5 hectares. We needed a public space that stitched the whole project together and allowed us to have a mix of uses. A bit like a Rockefeller Center kind of thing. We didn't know what the right scale was. We ended up actually taking a trip, with the office, to the MoMA. Part of our monthly art event, a sort of field trip. We were all sitting in the garden and were like, "Uh! This garden is a great scale." Because here is this space that somehow provides relief while you're in the middle of Midtown, surrounded by 40-story towers. So we studied the MoMA garden and replicated it nine times to create a network out of an object. So we stole a piece from the MoMA to breed as new urbanism.

WHITAKER (laughs) And you get to a point, in one courtyard, where you can start to see the next one.

ARNAIZ That's right. They're all engaged a little bit. Like the corner of one touches the corner of the other.

WHITAKER But you can also be in a place in the courtyard where you're just in the courtyard.

ARNAIZ That's right. And you don't notice that, when you get to the end, there's actually another one that goes through it.

WHITAKER Looking at that picture, I noticed all the arrows on the plan, because you're thinking through how people will use the space, and it reminds me of something I was thinking about earlier, when we started talking about communication and this question of composition. Because in a painting, you very much think about how the eye travels through the composition—sort of as a flat equivalent to how a person travels through the space. I think that's a huge part of design—or communication—signaling to someone where to start and then how to move from where they start. So if you look at a traditional French landscape painting, there's a point of entry. And the whole thing is never the same all over. It always has some things that are fuzzy and some things in detail. And I think the most successful pictures have a kind of electricity of making your eye move around them in a certain way.

The other thing I was thinking about was this notion of rules and social constructs and ways to behave in the French Academic tradition and how there's this tension between having rules and having freedom, where freedom can sometimes give you anxiety and rules can sometimes give you comfort. And I think that must be an interesting part of communicating how to use a space, when you want them to feel some sense of security and some sense of exploration.

ARNAIZ We typically start our project by saying, "The boundary of our site doesn't matter. We need to expand the boundary, have a sort of regional perspective and look at the stuff that's around us." That project in Bogotá, Colombia, it's an urban plan for the largest piece of open land left in Bogotá. We did this about one-month-long street analysis and buildings investigation, and found enormous heterogeneity. The edges were all quite different in spite of the fact that most people told us otherwise. Bogotá is a relatively well-organized city. It's on a grid, a numbered system based on the cardinal points around our site. All the grids were different, different in scale and different in orientation. So the biggest challenge was to design a grid that negotiated difference. It looks really simple, once it's done. A grid that actually took all of the grids from the neighborhoods and stitched them together without any expression of the stress, especially at the edge.

WHITAKER It's like taking a bunch of unsolved Rubik's Cubes and making them draw a line through a solved Rubik's Cube, in the middle matching up the little white cubes.

You're making me think, is this idea in communication about whether simplicity or complexity is more important? And maybe that you start with something that's very simple but then, to engage with this, you have to take a deep dive into the complexity of it. And the way that you're describing this, I think that this is an amazing, simple outcome of a highly complex process. But that there's something about the communication exercise of simplicity after complexity that I find really amazing and that, in this case, sort of speaks to a systems view of all these different pieces that come together. And I'm just wondering how you, as an architect or as a firm, relate to the idea of simplicity, how you see that as part of a, kind of, communication.

ARNAIZ (laughs)

WHITAKER Like, you know, are you suspicious of simplicity? Do you embrace it?

ARNAIZ It is a huge driver. It's certainly a big debate. On one hand, I think, like, my role in the office is the voice of simplicity. Because I'm sometimes outside of the projects. The designers are the ones that are really generating the stuff. But as a result of this proximity to the trees, they're so deep into the forest. They produce so much more complexity—good and bad.

WHITAKER Right. (laughter)

ARNAIZ And so an outsider's perspective enables one to ask, "How does this whole thing come together?—I don't understand this." "How do we communicate this?"

WHITAKER But I actually think that simplifying can be a profound act of synthesis, kind of pulling things together—

ARNAIZ Yeah. Exactly.

WHITAKER —and that there's a certain form of simplicity that is something where no one would have come up with it. It seems really evident when you see it but you wouldn't have come up with it ahead of time. You know, sort of like a concept in economics like comparative advantage. It's extremely simple but no one invented it for a very long time. So once you know it, you're like, "Of course." And that's maybe a measure of the, kind of, rightness of something, that it has an obviousness but never would have been inevitable ahead of time.

I think sometimes you can simplify up to the pattern, which can be a unique pattern of the project. Sometimes, you know, as you were saying, it's an act of being able to zoom out and see all the parts of something to understand the deep lines of the pattern. But I think sometimes it's the thing that you have to take out for the other pieces to fit together.

In entrepreneurship there is this idea of pivoting, where you kind of have to kick out one of the load-bearing walls to move forward. And I always think of it like you have a table with four legs and you're very invested in the four legs, because they're holding up the table of the idea. And the act of moving forward creatively is to kick out one of the legs, or two of the legs, and rotate the surface of the table onto another leg or another set of legs. It can be really hard to do, but then the new table can have a remarkable sturdiness you never imagined.

ARNAIZ That's brilliant. Yeah. That's such a wonderful way of describing it. And it also speaks to this question of no shortcuts. That act of discovery involves a lot of work, although the final thing might appear relaxed. The act of doing is so valuable—the process by which you move the table and kick the legs and discover that you never needed it at all.

WHITAKER Like how you know something or how you get to it is through an act of execution, which is often an act of conversation between your internal ideal of what might be possible and what actually can happen in the reality of the drawing or project. I just want to say that the idea of kicking the leg out, I think, comes partly from having read Annie Dillard's *The Writing Life*, which is about the process of writing and how the process of writing is different from something like the process of painting or drawing, where the words flow from left to right and so, at some point, you basically have to cut out all the words that got you started. And you're so grateful to them for getting you started. In a painting, they would be painted over or the file would be saved and you'd, you know, change or delete something. But she says that there's this stage where you realize there's a hairline fracture in the plot but to fix the hairline fracture requires kicking out the load-bearing walls, that you can save some favorite bricks but that's about it. Because I think there's a sort of secular/spiritual question of creative process, that has to do with being so completely and utterly committed to what you're working on and then having a non-graspy, non-attachment ability to put it aside and keep moving forward.

ARNAIZ Absolutely.

WHITAKER You know the Whistler quotation, "Industry is a necessity in the making of art but any evidence of it in the finished product should be considered a flaw"?

ARNAIZ Wow!

WHITAKER You're trying to show a process, but you're trying to show something that solves a problem and works, you know, in the present and in the future, in a space and time, not that shows how hard you worked to make it possible.

ARNAIZ One of our ambitions has been to produce a relaxed balance of infrastructure, one that is robust enough to allow for plural publics to emerge, to foster a new collective, yet not in a deterministic way, to force-feed a certain future. So there's a lot of looking, listening, and research.

WHITAKER There's that sort of Dultsky, *The Last Run of the Day* mentality. I think what you were just saying regarding the relaxed but robust infrastructure is really amazing. You're talking about creating an infrastructure that's not deterministic but somehow enabling, it seems. I think about it from the perspective of creative process and how you need containers for creative process. This idea of being a person in space is, in an everyday-life sense, a creative process of exploring and getting around. I think a container can be deeply, deeply enabling, if you can have autonomy in it, and then can be also highly constricting. One that syncs up to so many different concepts, communication being one of them. My mind is still really working through what you were saying much earlier, about what it is to build something in a place like Manila. I'm really kind of curious how you think about that.

ARNAIZ It's been quite interesting going back to these developing cities so frequently, over the last four years, since we started the office. I fly there every 45 days. And the contrast is so fascinating, coming back to New York, back to Brooklyn. Every time I return I am impressed by the amount of compounded realities that exist on top of each other in these developing cities. The contrast of social clusters is sometimes still difficult to kind of completely grasp. I think the cities there have become so kind—you know, *livable*, right? I am made to think of our obsession with livability in contemporary urban environments. The Bloomberg legacy for NYC is about a new urban gentility: bike paths, privately funded parks, and expanding museums. To some degree, none of that is in developing cities. I am trying to understand the emerging notion of the individual in that context. What is a person in this developing city? Realizing that residents in these cities are hyperaware of the outside world now. So the act of design is a kind of alchemical translation of the outside. We're trying to understand the ground but then we're also outside of it and we're bringing something in. We're like some weird alien form in there.

WHITAKER I'm thinking a lot about the process of observation as part of communication. I'm thinking about what you were saying about getting back to New York after your travels. And I'm thinking about that being so much a part of your world-view. And so this is a bit of a reductive thing to say, but when I think of systems thinking, I think of Donella Meadows and the kind of systems-thinking primer and stocks and flows but I also think about people like Elaine Scarry, who wrote about these plane crashes. And basically, that there's something to be said for the way that Western capitalism is structured around the object. It's the companies that make widgets. And a lot of these movements toward sustainability have this flavor of thinking about the context in which the widget is made and what the real costs are to the environment, et cetera. As David Foster Wallace said, a fish doesn't know what water is. Or if you ask people who come from Western societies or Eastern societies to look at a picture from under the surface of the ocean, probabilistically a Western-raised person is more likely to say, "There's a fish and there's a sea anemone," and someone else might describe the overall environment. And I'm just wondering if there's a way that you have an ability to riff off of the local structural language in part because of the way that you're coming to it, from, like, a personal history, as someone who's traveled among cultures and therefore has the ability to see the structure of the culture that you're living in in a way that a lot don't. And even when you're talking about the design of spaces and kind of breaking the edge of the space with the neighborhood, in these unstructured environments. Do you think some of that comes from your own personal . . . ?

ARNAIZ Well, I have to admit I've always been fascinated, even since college, with the figure of an exile, and so much so that actually, my final year at Williams, there was a professor in the literature department who I tapped and asked her if we could put together a course. Basically what we did was we looked at the figure of the exile in literature, meditating on why the exile, what the exile was doing, how the exile propelled the plot, how he or she related to her context in a different kind of way. So it's probably one of my continuing obsessions. (laughs) When people ask me, "Where are you from?" I don't really know anymore. I feel most at home in New York.

I guess we're all kind of a collection of exiles who are, sort of, happy here because of the creative freedom of this place. On a more procedural note, I do think that we at least try to foster and cultivate that figure of the exile when we're looking at problems. Perhaps it has to do with some discomfort, that we need to continually seek something that's not completely closed and that might allow us to keep on turning the table and kicking things.

WHITAKER I know that empathy is more universally accepted as a part of the design process, but I wonder if there's a form of radical empathy that comes from this exile perspective. Like when you talk about this discomfort, I wonder if it's related to being empathetic and trying to read yourself into the situation where you find yourself and also having an ability to place that on a larger ground, that you're not just trying to relate what they're doing to one local personal home but that you're seeing it in this very broad, almost existentially large context. I think there's a deep painfulness of being an exile. But there's some way that the lack of place gives you more flexibility or maneuverability or ability to kind of see things from an aerial point of view rather than a rooted, kind of first-person perspective.

ARNAIZ Maybe I'll answer it two ways. One is to agree with you that I think the exile, as a figure, is propelled by the reality of these shifting personalities, the looseness of the ground, the homelessness, and, somewhat, the pain of that. And the pain has a cognitive freedom that we try to channel into the way in which we look at problems and approach a project or approach people. But the other is also a comfort with desire, I would say. Because together with the exile's pain, there's their eroticism. The exile is also this figure who enjoys the bouncing around and takes joy in engaging in other people's parties and walking around new environments. To some degree, we're also about looking for ways in which we can create desire.

WHITAKER It's like a realized wanderlust—

ARNAIZ Yeah, that's right!

WHITAKER —the pleasure of a realized wanderlust. Maybe a kind of a poignancy, as opposed to a painfulness, like a nerve sensitivity to absorbing stimulus, for being a little bit unrooted.

—Recorded April 11, 2014

CONSTRUCTIONS

FRANK CALLAGHAN

CITY CENTER TOWER

HUE HOTEL

OCTOBER, 2015

IDEAS?
WE HAVE THE PERFECT VENUE TO SHOWCASE THEM.
SAFETY FIRST

IDEAS?
VENUE
TO SHOWCASE THEM
Let's Talk:

CAUTION CAUTION CAUTION CAUTION CAUTION CAUTION

CAUTION CAUTION CAUTION CAUTION CAUTION CAUTION CAUTION CAUTION CAUTION CAUTION CAUTION CAUTION

CAUTION
CAUTION

CAUTION
CAUTION
CAUTION
CAUTION

CAUTION

CAUTION

CAUTION

Taguig
BGC
Taguig

VERTICAL CLEARANCE 5.0M

RTICAL CLEARANCE 5.0M

PROJECT INDEX

STAFF AND PROJECT CREDITS

Carlos Arnaiz
Founder and Principal

USA
Laura del Pino
Senior Design Associate

Libo Li
Design Associate

Nutchanun Boontassaro
Designer

Jun Deng
Designer

Jingjun Li
Designer

Philippines
Monica Olbes
Executive Director

Kate Sarmiento
Associate

Colombia
Julián Bonilla
Partner

Mauricio Hurtado
Project Architect

SURBA
Peter Rowe
Co-founder

Chenghe Guan
Associate

100 Walls Church
Carlos Arnaiz, Principal
Laura del Pino, Senior Design Associate
Marc Leverant

Costa Rica Congress Hall
Carlos Arnaiz, Principal
Laura del Pino, Senior Design Associate

Cebu Transit
Carlos Arnaiz, Principal
Libo Li, Design Associate
Wayne Erb

House with Many Moons
Carlos Arnaiz, Principal
Nutchanun Boontassaro, Designer
Jessy Yang, Demitra Konstantinidis, Minkyung Song, Agathe Ceccaldi, Carlos Moya

Haishu Waterfront
Carlos Arnaiz, Principal
Minkyung Song

Hamilo Pavilion
Carlos Arnaiz, Principal
Laura del Pino, Senior Design Associate
Marc Leverant

Baler Hospital
Carlos Arnaiz, Principal
Libo Li, Design Associate
Wayne Erb, Marcos Cisneros

Lio Market Hall
Carlos Arnaiz, Principal
Alex Tseng

Tower One
Manila, Philippines
Carlos Arnaiz, Principal
Nutchanun Boontassaro, Designer
Laura del Pino, Senior Design Associate

Event Tent
Carlos Arnaiz, Principal
Jun Deng, Designer
Laura del Pino, Senior Design Associate
Agelica García

Frame House
Carlos Arnaiz, Principal
Laura del Pino, Senior Design Associate

La Salle Church
Carlos Arnaiz, Principal
Laura del Pino, Senior Design Associate
Tzu-Yin Wang, Alex Tseng

Bogota Centro
Carlos Arnaiz, Principal
Laura del Pino, Senior Design Associate
Demitra Konstantinidis

City Center Tower
Carlos Arnaiz, Principal
Jessy Yang, Tzu-Yin Wang

Hue Hotel
Carlos Arnaiz, Principal
Laura del Pino, Senior Design Associate
Shelby Ponce, Tzu-Yin Wang, Demitra Konstantinidis, Alex Tseng

CONTRIBUTORS

Iwan Baan is a Dutch architectural photographer.

Luke Bulman is director of Luke Bulman—Office.

Frank Callaghan is a photographer based in the Philipines.

Duks Koschitz is an assistant professor of architecture at Pratt Institute in New York

Phil Parker is an associate professor of architecture at Pratt Institute in New York

Peter Rowe is a principal of SURBA and former dean of Harvard University Graduate School of Design

Amy Whitaker is an Entrepreneur-in-Residence at the New Museum Incubator in New York.

PROFILE

CAZA

CAZA (Carlos Arnaiz Architects) is a Brooklyn-based design studio, workshop, and think tank with offices in Manila, Philippines, and Bogotá, Colombia. Our team consists of design professionals from around the world who envision an optimistic future for architectural thinking and informed experimentation. A collaborative office as committed to building as to the ideas that inform building, we believe that innovation inspires trust. Whether designing a bespoke residence, creating a master plan for a vibrant urban center, or rethinking how we work through an office building, we believe breakthroughs transform material culture into social expression. Our work represents an engagement with the history of making buildings and placing them in complex dynamic environments.

CAZA is currently developing a 450,000-square-meter mixed-use complex in Manila, a 90-hectare master plan for an emerging metropolitan district in China, and a large-scale civic development in Bogotá. Projects slated to open in 2016 include a hotel, an office tower, and a church. CAZA's design for the Taipei Contemporary Music Center, produced in collaboration with Office dA, was selected from among hundreds of entrants as one of three finalists to proceed to the second round of the competition, to contend for the contract to design and execute the project. CAZA has also been selected for inclusion in *50UNDER50* and *Architect Magazine*: Next Progressives; as a finalist for *ArchDaily*'s Best Buildings of the Year; and as a finalist in the *Architizer* A+ Awards for the 100 Walls Church.

SURBA

As the world continues to urbanize more opportunities and risks become manifest. The question is what do we make of them and how do we manage them toward sustainable qualities of life.

Who we are
We are a group of academics and professionals bringing unusual backgrounds, experiences, and insights to bear for the betterment of urban life.

What we do
We help people understand urbanization at various scales and across various topics as well as actively engaging with them in the creation of better places.

How we do it
We deploy analytical techniques that gain power and produce value through their application to geography, spatial planning, and urban design.

CAZA

Published on the occasion of CAZA's five-year anniversary, 2016

Copyediting
Kristin Kearns

Publicity
SUTTON
Noreen Ahmad
Julia Lukacher
Andrew Huff

Photograph, page 319, Ethan Hill
Photograph, page 64–65, Iwan Baan

Design
Luke Bulman—Office with Camille Sacha Salvador
lb-office.co

Printing
Regal Printing, Hong Kong

ISBN 978-1-223-223-3623

cazarch.com